30119 025 556 913

CITY

SA

D1151473

Thomas Cook

## WHAT'S IN YOUR GUIDEBOOK?

**Independent authors** Impartial up-to-date information from our travel experts who meticulously source local knowledge.

**Experience** Thomas Cook's 165 years in the travel industry and guidebook publishing enriches every word with expertise you can trust.

**Travel know-how** Thomas Cook has thousands of staff working around the globe, all living and breathing travel.

**Editors** Travel-publishing professionals, pulling everything together to craft a perfect blend of words, pictures, maps and design.

**You, the traveller** We deliver a practical, no-nonsense approach to information, geared to how you really use it.

# CITYSPOTS
# SALZBURG

**Written by Susi Cheshire**
**Updated by Bettina & Mike Lock**

**Published by Thomas Cook Publishing**
A division of Thomas Cook Tour Operations Limited
Company registration No: 1450464 England
The Thomas Cook Business Park, 9 Coningsby Road
Peterborough PE3 8SB, United Kingdom
Email: books@thomascook.com, Tel: +44 (0)1733 416477
www.thomascookpublishing.com

**Produced by The Content Works Ltd**
Aston Court, Kingsmead Business Park, Frederick Place
High Wycombe, Bucks HP11 1LA
www.thecontentworks.com

Series design based on an original concept by Studio 183 Limited

ISBN: 978-1-84848-059-9

Although every care has been taken in compiling this publication, and the contents
are believed to be correct at the time of printing, Thomas Cook Tour Operations
Limited cannot accept any responsibility for errors or omission, however caused,
or for changes in details given in the guidebook, or for the consequences of any
reliance on the information provided. Descriptions and assessments are based on
the author's views and experiences when writing and do not necessarily represent
those of Thomas Cook Tour Operations Limited.

# CONTENTS

## SYMBOLS KEY

The following symbols are used throughout this book:

ⓐ address ☎ telephone ⓦ website address ⓔ email
ⓛ opening times ⓝ public transport connections ⓘ important

The following symbols are used on the maps:

| | | | |
|---|---|---|---|
| 🄸 information office | | ▪ points of interest |
| ✈ airport | | O city |
| ✚ hospital | | O large town |
| 🛡 police station | | ○ small town |
| 🚌 bus station | | ══ motorway |
| 🚆 railway station | | ─ main road |
| ✝ cathedral | | ─ minor road |
| ❶ numbers denote featured cafés & restaurants | | ─ railway |

Hotels and restaurants are graded by approximate price as follows:
£ budget price ££ mid-range price £££ expensive

In addresses, 'Strasse' and '-strasse' (meaning 'street' or 'road')
are abbreviated to 'Str.' and '-str.'

◗ *Salzburg is dominated by beautiful baroque architecture*

# Introduction

Look beneath the marketing veneer of Mozart (born here in 1756) and *The Sound of Music* (filmed here in 1964), and you can get a real feel for life in this vibrant little city. Buildings with façades coloured like Battenberg cake line the River Salzach as it threads its way through the old centre of Salzburg and the forest-clad limestone mountains that flank it. The mountains' evocative names – Mönchsberg (Monks' Mountain), Nonnberg (Nuns' Mountain) and Kapuzinerberg (Capuchin Monks' Mountain) – reflect the rich monastic tradition of the area.

The people here represent a cocktail of chic and rustic charm, tradition and fun, and the city and surrounding area bursts with things to see and do. Take in some of the sights, absorb a bit of culture at some of the many concert halls, churches and art galleries (there are no less than 4,000 events per year), get an insight into the local customs, the country and its history, and take time out like the locals, relaxing in the traditional cafés or beer gardens. Beyond the tourist traps you'll find some fun and original places to eat and drink. Stroll around the woods up on Mönchsberg, walk along the river or in one of the parks, chill, enjoy the views, read... it's all up to you. If you just want pure, unadulterated natural beauty, take a day trip into the region around Salzburg and be inspired by its beautiful lake district, mysterious mountains and ice caves.

Salzburg manages to blend swirling baroque splendour with joyous kitsch, tradition with cool, the glory and grandeur of a rich princely past with the trappings of a tourist hotspot, and all of this within the framework of breathtaking mountain scenery, awe-inspiring culture, lakes, tranquillity and verdant alpine pastures. Few other small cities offer such diversity.

🔺 The baroque Pferdeschwemme (Horse Pond) is one of Salzburg's charms

# When to go

## SEASONS & CLIMATE

Salzburg has a wet reputation, thanks to the climatic impact of the close-lying Alps. The so-called *Schnürlregen* ('string rain') has become a cliché characterising the city and the feature of many a poem, book and operetta. But don't let rain dampen your mood; there is so much of Salzburg to see and discover indoors, and a walk around the city in the rain has a definite charm. Just don't forget to carry an umbrella and raincoat with you at all times; there is a reason why the 16th-century umbrella shop is still going strong.

The warm, Mediterranean-style climate can be tempting in summer, but high season means the city is packed with tourists. Unless you are going to Salzburg just for the concerts, you are best to avoid visiting during the famous *Festspiele* in July and

● *Classical performances resound from the Mozarteum*

August. At this time hotels and restaurants are fully booked and you won't get the best out of the rest of the city.

Spring is a fresh time to visit, especially May. September and October, however, are the best months, when the climate is most stable. Autumn gives the city a warm glow, there are fewer crowds, and you may be lucky enough to see some late summer sun. Winter is magical. It is very cold, but the crisp snow and bright sun make Salzburg an exciting destination around Christmas.

## ANNUAL EVENTS
### January
**Mozartwoche (Mozart Week)** falls between the end of January and the beginning of February. Salzburg celebrates its famous son with opera performances, classical concerts and often exhibitions too. Ⓦ www.mozarteum.at

### February
**Aspekte Salzburg** is a highbrow music festival featuring the work of contemporary European composers. Ⓦ www.aspekte-salzburg.at

### April
**Osterfestspiele**, one of the world's most famous international music and dance festivals, was founded in 1967. It features timeless operas, orchestral and choir concerts. The Berlin Philharmonic Orchestra performs here regularly. Ⓦ www.osterfestspiele-salzburg.at

### May
**Pfingsten & Barock (Whitsun & Baroque)** is another of

Salzburg's classical music festivals, including music by Bach.
ⓦ www.salzburgfestival.at

## June
**Sommer Szene (Summer Scene)**, from late June to mid-July,
celebrates young international contemporary artists in music and
the performing arts. ⓐ Anton-Neumayr-Platz 2 ⓣ 0662 843 711
ⓦ www.sommerszene.net

## July & August
**Festspiele** is the highlight of the festivals calendar. The famous
opera and classical music festival runs for five weeks in summer,
from late July to late August. ⓦ www.salzburgfestival.at

## September
**Rupertikirtag (St Rupert's Day)** is 24 September. Festivities take
place over five days, when a fairground is set up in the squares
around the cathedral to celebrate the patron saint of Salzburg.
Fairground rides, music, food and drink stalls, crafts and lots of
locals in traditional costume. ⓦ www.salzburg-altstadt.at

## October
**Kulturtage (Culture Days)** is another classical music, opera
and ballet festival held at various venues in mid-October.
ⓦ www.kulturvereinigung.com
**Jazz Herbst (Autumn Jazz Festival)** takes place from late October
to early November, when Austria's finest jazz stars are joined
by international performers in venues throughout the city.
ⓦ www.viennaentertainment.com

## November
**Adventsingen (Advent Singing)**, from the end of November through to mid-December, is a large, festive stage production in the Festspielhaus. ⓐ Residenzplatz 9 ⓣ 0662 843 182 ⓦ www.salzburgeradventsingen.at

## December
**Salzburg's Christmas markets** are a special treat. Enjoy mulled wine and roasted chestnuts while you search for gifts in Domplatz and Residenzplatz. Schloss Mirabell, the fortress and Hotel Stein's roof terrace are lit up beautifully.

### PUBLIC HOLIDAYS
**New Year's Day** 1 Jan
**Epiphany** 6 Jan
**Easter Monday** 13 Apr 2009; 5 Apr 2010; 25 Apr 2011
**Labour Day** 1 May
**Ascension Day** 21 May 2009; 13 May 2010; 2 June 2011
**Whit Monday** 1 June 2009; 24 May 2010; 13 June 2011
**Corpus Christi** 11 June 2009; 3 June 2010; 23 June 2011
**Assumption** 15 Aug
**National Day** 26 Oct
**All Saints' Day** 1 Nov
**Conception** 8 Dec
**Christmas Day** 25 Dec
**Boxing Day** 26 Dec

## Salzburg's *Festspiele*

Salzburg's main music event, the *Festspiele,* is the pinnacle of excellence in the classical and opera world. It takes place over five weeks from the end of July to the end of August. Dubbed a festival of superlatives, it draws the highest artistic talent from all corners of the globe as well as some 220,000 visitors. Over 170 performances are given by world-renowned artists, who provide a rich and varied programme of theatre and opera. The whole event takes an enormous amount of preparation. Performances are mainly staged in three of the festival halls, the Festspielhaus, the Haus für Mozart and the Felsenreitschule.

During the festival, an air of opulence, tradition and rich cultural flair descends on the city. If you want to experience all this, Salzburg at festival time is worth the visit and you'll be treated to an unforgettable time of your life. But be warned; the city will feel full to bursting and it will be hard to find a room, let alone a table in a nice restaurant. The influx of visitors tends to push prices higher, too, and even the demure little airport swarms with private jets like a honeypot invaded by bees. Salzburg becomes the central focus of the opera and theatre world for five weeks a year, and for some, the baroque city suffers somewhat from a rather over-inflated ego for the duration.

The festival programme is announced on the website the previous November, along with booking details. The annual opening feature is *Jedermann*, performed on an open stage in Domplatz, just as in 1920 when it all began. Tickets to most performances are hard to come by and very expensive, often block-booked, so you need to decide what you want to see well in advance. Ⓦ www.salzburgfestival.at

◆ *Enjoy a concert during the* Festspiele *at the* Festspielhaus

# History

It all started with *Salz* (salt), the so-called white gold that gave the city its name. The mining of salt led to trade and a late Stone Age settlement on the river. Celts also swept through the area, and in AD 51–54 the Romans bestowed a municipal charter on Juvavum, the town on their main trade route through Europe. Before long a monastic community was set up, establishing the city's religious roots.

The figure considered to be Salzburg's founder is St Rupert. He arrived around 700 and built St Peter's church and monastery as well as the Nonnberg convent. The famous St Peter's restaurant dates back to 803.

Salzburg went through a rich period under Charlemagne as the seat of the Bavarian dukes, hosting important bishops and archbishops and becoming an independent ecclesiastical principality. After the German Emperor Barbarossa burned the city to the ground in 1167, there followed a surge of reconstruction under the prince-archbishops between the 13th and 17th centuries. Trade and the arts flourished.

Three key names who really made their mark in the 17th century are the archbishops Wolf Dietrich, Markus Sittikus and Paris Lodron. They built the baroque city as it is today. It was even dubbed 'Rome of the North' for its Italianate flair. Sittikus also built the summer palace, Schloss Hellbrunn, while the university took Lodron's name.

In 1756 Wolfgang Amadeus Mozart was born into the affluent German Catholic principality of Salzburg. The city was in a state of change, however. Church reforms were taking place and feudalism was being questioned. Social boundaries were dissolving and Enlightenment intellectualism was creeping through the middle classes, enabling Mozart to become independent and freelance rather than having to work for the court. But he still felt stifled and left for Vienna in 1781. In 1816 Salzburg became part of the Austrian Habsburg Empire.

The year 1920 saw the first Salzburg Festival, which established the city as a key centre for arts of the highest standard. It starts in July every year and lasts for five weeks.

Salzburg developed its role as an important trade centre during World War II, later becoming a key tourist destination renowned for its culture and beautiful natural surroundings. The famous Hollywood film *The Sound of Music,* filmed here in 1964, offered yet another possibility for attracting tourists that was – and continues to be – expertly exploited. In 1989 the last salt was extracted from a nearby mine, and UNESCO declared the Altstadt (Old Town) a world heritage site in 1997.

Anywhere with a history as glorious as Salzburg's runs the risk of becoming stuck in the past, but that has not happened to this city. Today, tourism continues to flourish and Salzburg still manages to balance its ecclesiastical baroque heritage and folkloric tradition with ever more contemporary art and architecture. Following its spectacular success as a host city of 2008's European Football Championships, Salzburg's profile as a major destination has been justifiably raised. For this city with a dazzling past, the future looks bright indeed.

# Lifestyle

Salzburgers are proud of their genius son Mozart, but aren't so keen on the tasteless, over-marketed image plastered all over souvenirs. A cultured bunch, they love classical music and art, and their city is a magnet drawing the rich and famous to its *Festspiele* concerts every summer. Unfortunately, this sends the cost of living soaring, so many locals are moving further away from the city centre.

People in Salzburg are proud of their traditions and love a good excuse to slip into traditional costumes, *Trachten*. These are becoming fashionable again for the younger Salzburgers, who dress up for festivals, weddings and other formal occasions. The women wear a white blouse with a tight bodice over the top, plus a *dirndl* skirt and apron. The men wear a checked shirt and *Lederhosen*, with an alpine-style wool or suede jacket with horn buttons. You can tell the marital status of a woman by the position of her apron bow; it's tied on the right if she's married, in the middle if she's widowed, and on the left if she is still single.

Austrians take great pride in their appearance in general, and dress is elegant and fairly conservative, as is behaviour. First names are not often used in business, and you will always be greeted with your last name and preceding title, such as Herr (Mr), Frau (Mrs) or Fräulein (Miss).

Salzburgers generally love to be active and certainly make the most of living close to mountains and lakes. In the early evenings and at weekends you can see locals enjoying their free time and relaxing outdoors. The paths along the River Salzach and through the woods on Mönchsberg or in the Hellbrunn grounds often fill up with joggers and cyclists. Hiking is a favourite pastime. In summer many also head to the lakes for a quick dip after work, and in winter they hit the nearby ski slopes and are home in time for supper.

🔺 *Salzburg's alpine setting*

# Culture

Known as a world stage, Salzburg is steeped in culture, and music is a big part of life. Throughout the year there are a great number of festivals and performances of classical music, jazz, theatre, opera and ballet. Some of the best venues for visitors include the Festung Hohensalzburg (Hohensalzburg Fortress) and Schloss Mirabell's Marble Hall, the only palace room open to the public. Both hold special concerts on a regular basis. The recently renovated Mozarteum University of Music and Dramatic Arts hosts numerous operas in its concert hall during the five to six weeks of the summer festival, when the world's best performers descend on the city (see page 14). The true sound of music can often be heard coming from their hotel rooms or through festival hall windows during rehearsals.

Real classical treats are the visiting Berlin Philharmonic Orchestra under Simon Rattle at the *Osterfestspiele* (Easter Festival), the Camerata Salzburg Orchestra, and the Mozarteum Orchestra. Mozart's music can be heard all over Salzburg and there is also an excellent choice of CDs available in many good music shops in the city.

Though the theatre and classical concert scene remains traditional, the city is becoming more open to contemporary design, art and architecture. Art is surprisingly avant-garde for this pretty baroque city. The number of art venues, good private galleries and museums increases every year in the city and currently totals over 80. Several young, forward-thinking people are introducing more art to hotels, cafés and venues, and the Museum der Moderne (Museum of Modern Art) has a bold new

◆ *A statue of Salzburg's most famous son, Mozart*

director. Once a year on a Saturday in autumn the national TV channel ORF sponsors a nationwide *Lange Nacht der Museen* (open night for museums). The Salzburg Foundation is an organisation commissioning permanent artwork under the Salzburg Art Project from an internationally renowned artist every year, such as Anselm Kiefer. Even contemporary and daring architectural designs are being embraced, such as Volkmar Burgstaller's Hangar-7 (a futuristic tourist attraction with a hip bar, high-class restaurant and display space for Dietrich Mateschitz's collection of aeroplanes) and his Hotel Schloss Mönchstein restaurant, Matteo Thun's Museum der Moderne restaurant M32, and Massimiliano Fuksas' Europark shopping centre.

Literature lovers should head to the Literaturhaus, an important centre for writers who were born or lived in Salzburg, including Georg Trakl, Stefan Zweig, Carl Zuckmayer, Thomas Bernhard, Peter Handke and Karl-Markus Gauss. The members offer readings (in German) and articles on contemporary authors, as well as bike tours that take in the main spots mentioned in literature written about Salzburg.

● *Cross the bridge from the New Town to the Old Town*

# MAKING THE MOST OF
Salzburg

# Shopping

Shopping is a delight in Salzburg's pedestrianised Old Town. All the small, traditional, old-fashioned speciality shops can be found along Getreidegasse, Griesgasse, Goldgasse and Alter Markt on the left bank, as well as Linzer Gasse and Dreifaltigkeitsgasse on the right bank. The shops have kept their original façades and on Getreidegasse they all display traditional iron signs. The original signs are the most charming but you can see a Zara and a McDonald's there too.

Markets can be fun and lively, and usually sell fruit, vegetables, souvenirs and handicrafts. Head to Universitätsplatz on Mondays to Saturdays and Mirabellplatz on Thursdays. Along Elisabethkai on the right bank of the Salzach you'll find an arts and crafts market every second weekend in summer.

If you want a modern shopping centre, take Bus 1 from the central bus station to the state-of-the-art Europark in the Klessheim area of Salzburg. It has a wealth of international mid-market clothing brands, cafés, a cinema and a kids' club.

Most supermarkets are further out of town, but the following are conveniently located:

**Billa** ⓐ Griesgasse 19–21 Ⓝ Bus: 18, 24
**Billa** ⓐ Rainerstr. 19–23 (near Hauptbahnhof) Ⓝ Bus: 1, 3, 5, 6
**Billa** ⓐ Maxglaner Hauptstr. 18 (near Stiegl Brauwelt) Ⓝ Bus: 1
**Hofer** ⓐ Innsbrucker Bundesstr. 112 Ⓝ Bus: 2

If you're looking for something to take home, then the ubiquitous *Mozartkugeln* (Mozart balls), local chocolate-coated sweets filled with pistachio marzipan and praline, make great gifts. Only the silver and blue wrapped ones are the originals.

⬥ *Window-shopping along the Getreidegasse*

## USEFUL SHOPPING PHRASES

**What time do the shops open/close?**
Um wieviel Uhr öffnen/schließen die Geschäfte?
*Oom veefeel oor erffnen/shleessen dee geshefter?*

**How much is this?**
Wieviel kostet das?
*Veefeel kostet das?*

**Can I try this on?**
Kann ich das anprobieren?
*Can ikh das anprobeeren?*

**My size is ...**
Ich habe Größe ...
*Ikh haber grerser ...*

**I'll take this one, thank you**
Ich nehme das, danke schön
*Ikh neymer das, danker shern*

**This is too large/too small/too expensive**
Es ist zu groß/zu klein/zu teuer
*Es ist tsu gross/tsu kline/tsu toyer*

The original producer, Fürst, has three shops and a café in town.

Another speciality is *Trachten* (traditional costumes). Due to their popularity among the locals, there are several shops in Salzburg which still make them.

Wines, beers and especially schnapps are also good gifts and things to take home. Schnapps made from rowanberries or pine kernels is the local speciality.

# Eating & drinking

Salzburg has a rich gastronomic history influenced by the opulent periods of its history, its trade and its monastic past. The various gourmet temples are kept on their toes with the annual influx of prominent guests and stars during the summer *Festspiele*. Among the 500 places to eat in the city, there are several international restaurants, including Italian, Mexican and Chinese.

Typical Austrian food is meaty and traditional with rustic Hungarian and Bohemian influences, resulting in such hearty fare as broths, meat strudel, meat with noodles and vegetables, and *Knödel* (dumplings). Common dishes are *Gulasch* (goulash), *Tafelspitz* (slices of boiled beef with roast potatoes, vegetables and chive sauce), *Backhuhn* (chicken baked in breadcrumbs), and *Wiener Schnitzel* (a thinly battered slice of veal in breadcrumbs). Game such as venison, duck, pheasant and goose is also popular in season. Fresh, locally caught fish is another speciality in the region. Look for *Saibling* (char), *Forelle* (trout) and *Zander* (pike-perch).

You cannot leave without trying the *Salzburger Nockerl* (sweet soufflé). It's sweet, huge and very rich. One serving is enough for four. It is always freshly baked, so bring to the table a little patience and a big appetite. It is a soufflé whipped into three large peaks,

### PRICE CATEGORIES
The following price categories used in this book indicate the average cost of a three-course meal without drinks:
**£** up to €15   **££** €15–30   **£££** over €30

signifying the three Salzburg mountains, baked to a golden brown, sprinkled with icing sugar and served on a silver platter. This time-consuming and delicate process of preparation means it has disappeared from many menus. The best place to taste it is St Peter's.

Traditional coffee houses are another Austrian speciality. Two of the most famous in Salzburg are Café Tomaselli on the left bank and Café Bazar on the right. Vienna's famous Sacher Hotel also made a second home here. Sample their magnificent chocolate cake (*Sachertorte*), homemade to the original princely recipe of 1832.

Then there's the beer. Beer gardens are plentiful and very welcoming in summer and autumn. A long-standing establishment in Salzburg culture and one of the largest beer cellars in Europe is the Augustinerbräu. Here you can join the locals in the beer garden under great horse chestnut trees, grown to provide cool shade for the beer stores in cellars directly underground. Enjoy a stone mug of strong, cold beer. You can even bring your own food, so long as you buy the beer here. The Stieglkeller is the other famous old brewery in Salzburg, with a beer garden boasting fabulous views over the city.

Restaurant etiquette is similar to that in the rest of Europe, with no strict dos and don'ts. Dress is fairly casual but smart; don't turn up to a high-class restaurant in shorts, but jeans and a smart jacket are acceptable. Overly revealing women's summer tops are frowned upon. In terms of tipping, it is standard to round the smaller amounts for a drink, for example, up to the nearest 50 cents or euro. Average tipping for restaurant bills is 5–10 per cent.

If you're in a truly casual mood, Salzburg offers loads of parks and open spaces where you can picnic. Join the locals in Hellbrunn

Park, Mirabell Gardens or just alongside the river. Supermarkets are not a common sight in the centre of the Old Town, so make the most of the small shops and get provisions from the many bakers, delicatessens and markets. If you are out of the centre, Spar, Billa, Zielpunkt and Hofer are the supermarket chains to look out for. The best markets are:

**Green Market** ⓐ Universitätsplatz ⓒ 07.00–19.00 Mon–Fri, 07.00–15.00 Sat

**Schranne** ⓐ Mirabellplatz ⓒ 05.00–13.00 Thur

◗ *Enjoy a coffee on the terrace of Café Tomaselli*

## USEFUL DINING PHRASES

**I would like a table for ... people, please**
Ich möchte ein Tisch für ... Personen, bitte
*Ikh merkhter ine teesh foor ... perzohnen, bitter*

**Waiter/waitress!**
Herr Ober/Frau Kellnerin!
*Hair ohber/frow kell-nair-in!*

**May I have the bill, please?**
Die Rechnung, bitte?
*Dee rekhnung, bitter?*

**I am a vegetarian. Does this contain meat?**
Ich bin Vegetarier (Vegetarierin fem.). Enthält das hier Fleisch?
*Ish bin veggetaareer (veggetaareerin). Enthelt dass heer flyshe?*

**Where is the toilet (restroom) please?**
Wo sind die Toiletten, bitte?
*Voo zeent dee toletten, bitter?*

**I would like a cup of/two cups of/another coffee/tea, please**
Ich möchte eine Tasse/zwei Tassen/noch eine Tasse Kaffee/Tee, bitte
*Ikh merkhter iner tasser/tsvy tassen/nok iner tasser kafey/tey, bitter*

**I would like a beer/two beers, please**
Ich möchte ein Bier/Zwei Biere, bitte
*Ikh merkhter ine beer/tsvy beerer, bitter*

# Entertainment & nightlife

Salzburg offers a variety of fun and contemporary places to visit in the evening. There are some great bars with music and views, simple traditional beer gardens and sophisticated wine bars, as well as classical theatres, alternative venues, dinner with music, or films in their original language. The only problem you will have is deciding what to do.

In terms of musical and operatic performances, there is something on every evening, from a concert in a church to a performance in the Mozarteum concert hall. The Mozart Dinner and the **Sound of Salzburg Show** (❶ 0662 826 617 Ⓦ www.soundofsalzburgshow.com Ⓛ Dinner & show: 19.30–22.00 mid-May–mid-Oct; show only: 20.30–22.00 mid-May–mid-Oct) offer a unique evening's entertainment and are held regularly. The Mozart Dinner is a sophisticated affair with arias and duets performed between courses, and the Sound of Salzburg Show is a fun, cheesy sing-along complete with film clips of the real Maria von Trapp. Your hotel or the Tourist Board can help you book these and other concert tickets, and provide you with a calendar of musical events. If you want to plan ahead before you travel, check Ⓦ www.salzburg.info and Ⓦ www.salzburgfestival.at

Good music venues for various gigs are Rock House (see page 90), Jazzit (see page 90) and ARGEKultur (see page 104). International bands or solo artists on tour play at the Salzburg Arena. During the festivals, many venues around the city offer evening performances. **Frequency** is an annual open-air festival which hosts the latest cult bands in the Salzburgerring venue

Spin the wheels until 3am at Casino Salzburg

at Fuschlsee, a lake nearby. See ⓦ www.frequency.at or
ⓦ www.musicticket.at for details.

Classical theatre is what Salzburg specialises in, but there is
an alternative scene too. As well as the music, ARGEKultur offers
contemporary dance and theatre performances (in German).

For clubs and bars, the Tourist Board may recommend Rupertkai
as the nightlife mile. However, locals will advise you to head to more
stylish and sophisticated venues. Rupertkai has developed a bad
reputation for alcopop-fuelled violence in the early hours. Measures
are in place to clean up the area's image, so things may improve.

If the casino is your thing, head out to Schloss Klessheim
in Wals outside the city. You can catch a free shuttle bus from
Mirabellplatz. See ⓦ www.casinos.at for more details.

Das Kino cinema on the riverside shows some films in their
original language, so check their programme if you feel like sitting
back and enjoying a movie without subtitles. They have alternative,
art-house and children's films too.

You can find out about events from various publications
and brochures, and most hotels have a plethora of free leaflets.
Unfortunately, there are no English 'what's on' publications. The
*Salzburger Nachrichten* paper (on sale in kiosks) lists what's on daily
in German, and in English on its website (ⓦ www.salzburg.com).
Event listings in German can be found in the booklets *Salzburger
Wochenspiegel* (on sale in kiosks), the *Veranstaltungen Events
Manefestazioni* with introductions in English (free from tourist
information offices), and *ES, Das Erlebe Salzburg Magazin* (free in
bars, cafés and venues). Tickets may be booked at the following:
**Salzburger Nachrichten** has its own online ticket centre.
ⓦ www.salzburg.com/ticketcenter

**Salzburg Ticket Service** is situated within the tourist information office. ⓐ Mozartplatz 5 ⓣ 0662 840 310 ⓦ http://en.salzburgticket.com

**Ticketcenter Polzer** ⓐ Residenzplatz 3 ⓣ 0662 8969 ⓦ www.polzer.com

● A great way to get round the city is by bike

# Sport & relaxation

## SPECTATOR SPORTS
### Salzburg Arena
This venue holds the major four-day show-jumping tournament, Amadeus Horse Indoors, in October (ⓦ www.amadeushorseindoors.at), and the Motocross Freestyle show in December. ⓐ Am Messezentrum 1, A-5020 Salzburg ⓣ 0662 240 40 ⓦ www.salzburgarena.at

## PARTICIPATION SPORTS
### Cycling
Cycling is big in Salzburg, and cycle paths are well kept and safe, running through parks and along the river. Two good bike hire shops are:

**Citybike** Fifteen bikes locked into units which are freed once you enter your details on the touch screen. Pay about €1 to register. Your credit card is debited on your return. ⓐ Hanuschplatz ⓦ www.citybikesalzburg.at

**Top Bike** Along with bikes, they also offer self-guided bike tours and crazy 'Octopus conference-bikes' for up to seven people. ⓐ Hauptbahnhof, Südtiroler Platz 1; Staatsbrücke, Franz-Josef-Kai ⓦ www.topbike.at

### Snow sports
Daily from mid-December to mid-March, the Salzburg Tourismus winter snow shuttle bus travels to the nearby hills. You can get to Gastein, Zell am See or Kitzbühel for skiing, snowboarding, tobogganing or cross-country skiing.

**Salzburg Tourismus** ☎ 0662 871 712 (reservations)
ⓔ snowshuttle@salzburg.info ⏱ 08.30 from Mirabellplatz

### Spa & fitness
**Holmes Place** offers fitness facilities, spas, pool, salon, crèche,
restaurant and parking. Daily membership available. ⓐ Innsbrucker
Bundesstr. 35 ☎ 0662 4249 9090 ⓦ www.holmesplace.at
⏱ 07.00–23.00 Mon–Thur, 07.00–22.00 Fri, 09.00–21.30 Sat

### Swimming
**Paracelsus** swimming baths have a 15 x 25 m (49 x 82 ft)
heated indoor pool with huge windows overlooking Mirabell
Gardens, a climbing wall, diving tower, saunas and kids' adventure
pool. In summer try the open-air pools (see page 134). **Paracelsus**
ⓐ Auerspergstr. 2 ☎ 0662 883 544 ⓦ www.paracelsusbad.at
⏱ 10.00–20.00 Mon–Fri, 10.00–19.00 Sat & Sun. Admission charge

### Walking & hiking
Within minutes you can be on Mönchsberg or Kapuzinerberg,
surrounded by woods and fantastic views. Further afield is the
1,280 m (4,199 ft) Gaisberg, a mountain paradise for hikers.
**Gaisberg** ⓦ Bus: 6 (Mirabellplatz), 7 (Ludwig-Schmederer-Platz),
4 (Josef-Kaut-Str. & Valkenauerstr.)

# Accommodation

Accommodation in Salzburg offers great variety, from humble youth hostels, campsites and B&Bs, to stylish, design-conscious hotels and a handful of luxury 5-stars. There are over 130 hotels, 5 hostels and 4 campsites, so you're rather spoilt for choice. A large number of classic hotels were built in the 19th century on the left bank, and these have been well renovated. The right bank boasts several well-known hotel chains. All central hotels are well signed and within easy walking distance of the main sights. If you look a little further out on the edges of town, there are some more affordable places to stay with excellent and easy bus links to the centre. If you are a family with children, and are looking for something a little different, you could opt for a few days' stay at one of 320 working farms in the region (ⓦ www.salzburg.farmholidays.com).

Costs are on a par with other European cities, but the difference here is that the festival weeks at various times throughout the year get booked up well in advance, so pick your time carefully and plan ahead. Arriving without accommodation shouldn't be problematic out of high season, say in spring or late autumn, as long as you avoid the festival weeks. In summer and winter,

**PRICE CATEGORIES**
The ratings below indicate the approximate cost of a double room per night, including breakfast:
£ up to €100   ££ €100–200   £££ over €200

however, you definitely need to book to avoid disappointment.

**Tourismus Salzburg** offers an excellent service, booking rooms for a nominal fee via email and on their website. The website gives the contact details of all accommodation registered, so you can also choose to book directly with the hotel. ❶ 0662 8898 7314 ⓦ www.salzburg.info

## HOTELS

**AllYouNeed Hotel Salzburg £** Only open July to Sept but offers very competitive rates and basic rooms. ⓐ Glockengasse 4B (Right bank Altstadt) ❶ 01 512 7493 (out of season), 0662 875 159 (July–Sept) ⓦ www.allyouneedhotels.at ⓝ Bus: 4

**Zur Post £–££** Out of the centre, 20 minutes by foot and a short hop on the bus, this place constitutes three linked houses and a central garden. ⓐ Maxglaner Hauptstr. 45 (Mönchsberg, Nonnberg & beyond) ❶ 0662 8323 390 ⓦ www.hotelzurpostsalzburg.at ⓝ Bus: 1

**Altstadthotel Amadeus ££** Very family friendly, this has modern flair in a traditional house close to shops and restaurants. ⓐ Linzer Gasse 43–45 (Left bank Altstadt) ❶ 0662 871 401 ⓦ www.hotelamadeus.at

**Altstadthotel Stadtkrug ££** Full of traditional charm. You can walk up the Kapuzinerberg from here or enjoy the shops at your doorstep. ⓐ Linzer Gasse 20 (Left bank Altstadt) ❶ 0662 873 545 ⓦ www.stadtkrug.at

◔ *The arty-yet-homely Arthotel Blaue Gans*

**Goldene Ente ££** You can't beat this central location in a narrow old street. Stylish rooms with historical touches and a great restaurant. ⓐ Goldgasse 10 (Left bank Altstadt) ⓣ 0662 845 622 ⓦ www.ente.at

**Mozart ££** This right bank hotel is close to all the sights and transport links. Pleasant, family-run and traditional classic décor. ⓐ Franz-Josef-Str. 27 (Right bank Altstadt) ⓣ 0662 872 274 ⓦ www.hotel-mozart.at

**Arthotel Blaue Gans ££–£££** Central and stylish with a fabulous bar, restaurant and terrace café, friendly staff and plenty of contemporary art. ⓐ Getreidegasse 41–43 (Left bank Altstadt) ⓣ 0662 8424 910 ⓦ www.blauegans.at

**Austria Trend Hotel Europa ££–£££** Located right by the main station. A modern chain hotel with good business facilities. ⓐ Rainerstr. 31 (Right bank Altstadt) ⓣ 0662 889 930 ⓦ www.austria-trend.at/eus

**Hotel Stein ££–£££** Popular roof restaurant and terrace with great food, wines and the best view. Cosy, sleekly modern rooms with atmospheric low lighting. On a busy riverside road. ⓐ Giselakai 3–5 (Right bank Altstadt) ⓣ 0662 8743 460 ⓦ www.hotelstein.at

**Schloss Mönchstein £££** A luxury hideaway up on the mountain overlooking the city. There's even a futuristic spherical glass restaurant and underground spa. If you're going to blow the budget, do it in style. ⓐ Mönchsberg Park 26 (Mönchsberg, Nonnberg & beyond) ⓣ 0662 8485 550 ⓦ www.monchstein.at

## HOSTELS & GUESTHOUSES

**Jugend & Familiengästehaus Salzburg** £ Not too far from the centre, in Nonnberg, with internet café and park. ⓐ Josef-Preis-Allee 18 (Mönchsberg, Nonnberg & beyond) ⓣ 0662 8426 700 ⓦ www.jfgh.at

**Naturfreundehaus Stadtalm** £ Amazing quiet location up on Mönchsberg. Basic and small, with a lovely café with views. ⓐ Gruber&Esterer OEG, Mönchsberg 19C (Mönchsberg, Nonnberg & beyond) ⓣ 0662 841 729 ⓔ ng.esterer@utanet.at

**Pension Ebner** £ Pleasant family home with guest rooms, near the airport. ⓐ Innsbrucker Bundesstr. 77A (Mönchsberg, Nonnberg & beyond) ⓣ 0662 827 563 ⓝ Bus: 2

**Yoho Salzburg Hostel** £ Single, group or family rooms available. Central location on the right bank. ⓐ Paracelsusstr. 9 (Right bank Altstadt) ⓣ 0662 879 649 ⓦ www.yoho.at

## CAMPSITES

**Camping Nord-Sam** £ Located north of the town. A big plus is its swimming pool. Open from April to late September. ⓐ Samstr. 22A ⓣ 0662 660 494 ⓦ www.camping-nord-sam.com ⓝ Bus: 23

**Camping Schloss Aigen** £ On the edges of town in wonderful parkland. It has a restaurant and shop. ⓐ Weberbartlweg 20 ⓣ 0662 622 079 ⓦ www.campingaigen.com ⓝ Bus: 7

# THE BEST OF SALZBURG

Whether you are on a flying visit to Salzburg, or taking a more leisurely break in Austria, the city offers some sights and experiences that should not be missed.

## TOP 10 ATTRACTIONS

- **The Sound of Music** Concerts and world-class music festivals vie with the fame of the Von Trapp family (see page 20)

- **Mozart's houses** Learn about the genius's life, family and work (see pages 65 & 80)

- **Contemporary and avant-garde art** In the fabulous Rupertinum, Artmosphere and Mönchsberg Museum der Moderne (see pages 68 & 99)

- **Hangar-7** An aeroplane museum and very cool gastronomic hang-out (see page 46)

- **Schloss Mirabell** Get a feel for Salzburg's stately past in the grounds of this beautiful palace (see page 80)

- **Local brew** Soak up the local atmosphere in the Augustinerbräu or Stieglkeller beer gardens (see pages 103 & 104)

- **Festung Hohensalzburg (Hohensalzburg Fortress)** Enjoy fabulous views from the terrace café and be gruesomely impressed by the torture chamber (see page 93)

- **Café culture** Indulge yourself with local delicacies from one of the city's 80 cafés (see page 28)

- **Strolling** You'll never tire of wandering through the squares and narrow streets, past fountains, baroque and rococo façades and along the river (see page 46)

- **Barockmuseum (Baroque Museum)** Gain insight into Salzburg's extravagant past (see page 81)

⬥ *The beautiful Mirabell Gardens*

# Suggested itineraries

## HALF-DAY: SALZBURG IN A HURRY

To get the best out of the city in a few hours take to the streets. Walk the length of the Old Town on the left bank past churches, shops and around the cathedral squares. Alternatively, take the lift up to Mönchsberg, enjoy the views, and walk down to the city passing the Stieglkeller beer garden, the cathedral, St Peter's cemetery, Sigmund-Haffner-Gasse and Alter Markt, and finish with a stroll along Getreidegasse.

## 1 DAY: TIME TO SEE A LITTLE MORE

Start off in Café Tomaselli on the left bank, visit some shops, then head over to the right bank on Makartsteg bridge. Wander through Mirabell Gardens and see the contemporary art in Thaddaeus Ropac's gallery, head down Berggasse and up Kapuzinerberg. Back in town, visit the Stein Hotel's roof terrace for a break and amazing views over the left bank, wander around inside the Dom (cathedral) and Mozarts Geburtshaus (Mozart's birthplace), take the Festspielhaus tour after lunch and sneak a peek at the Pferdeschwemme (Horse Pond). Dine nearby in the Blaue Gans, a contemporary take on an old inn.

## 2–3 DAYS: TIME TO SEE MUCH MORE

With a bit more time, you'll be able to do everything listed above in more depth, plus take a trip out to Hellbrunn to see how the former prince entertained his guests in his summer palace and grounds. You could spend a whole day here, then return for a classical concert and a traditional Salzburg dinner in the Festung Hohensalzburg or St Peter's Stiftskeller restaurant. Alternatively, if you are a *Sound of Music* fan, join the four-hour organised Panorama tour taking in the lakes and various beautiful film locations. In the evening, visit the Sternbräu's Sound of Salzburg dinner show and relive the film moments with a sing-along.

## LONGER: ENJOYING SALZBURG TO THE FULL

With more time to spare you can do all of the above and explore the mountains, villages, lakes, ice caves and salt mines in the Salzkammergut region surrounding the city.

◗ *At Mirabell Palace you may find yourself singing 'My Favourite Things'*

# Something for nothing

For such a richly cultural city, there is a surprising amount you can do for free. Simply walk around, without going into the buildings with admission charges, and you will get a real feel for this historic city. If you want to make the most of the city on a tight budget, consider purchasing a Salzburg Card which gets you into all the sights for free and on all the buses too. You can travel as far as the beautiful Schloss Hellbrunn with this card, by bus or boat. Enjoy a picnic in the park, the trick water fountains and palace.

Salzburg is in many ways defined by its religious background and there are numerous churches, each with its own treasures or works of religious art. Organ, choir and instrumental classical music is an integral part of Sunday services in the churches, so find out beforehand what's on offer and make sure you get there early to get a seat. Choose from the Dom (Cathedral), Franziskanerkirche (Franciscan Church), St Peter's, Mülln, Nonnberg and Universitätskirche (University Church). Information on all of these can be found at tourist information offices, your hotel, the daily paper *Salzburger Nachrichten* (Ⓦ www.salzburg.com/sn), and the German website Ⓦ www.kirchen.net/kirchenmusik

Walks on Mönchsberg and Kapuzinerberg are wonderful ways to enjoy the natural beauty of the region. You can also spend an hour or two strolling around the woods either side of the river. If you're feeling more adventurous, hike up the Gaisberg (see page 36).

On a more contemporary note, Hangar-7, near the airport, has free entry and includes the Red Bull Flying Bulls transport exhibition. From the Red Bull Formula One racing car to an Alpha Jet, a silver B25 and old yellow Piper Aircraft plane, it's all here under one steel and glass roof. The building alone is worth visiting for its amazing architectural structure, and it's all just a cheap bus ride (Bus 2) from town.

⬤ *The free-to-enter Mirabell Gardens have much to amuse*

# When it rains

Rain falls regularly in Salzburg, but it can provide a nice excuse to explore more places indoors or to take longer over your morning coffee in one of the famous coffee houses. Whichever side of the river you are on, the shops are all enticing and provide a delightful way to spend a few hours, whether you're gift-buying or just browsing. Salzburg is renowned for its charming little traditional boutiques and handicraft stores. You can find out more about traditional *Trachten* costumes at the Gwandhaus in Nonntal or the Beurle store on Griesgasse, where small exhibitions explain the details and history of these colourful outfits.

On the right bank, in the Neue Residenz building on Mozartplatz, the **Carolino Augusteum Museum** (ⓦ www.smca.at) is a good place to find out more about Salzburg's rich past and see some fascinating treasures. The Haus der Natur (Natural History Museum, see page 134), near the Mönchsberg lift, is another fun activity when rain stops play. You can spend hours looking at the reptiles and dinosaurs or scientific, astrological, meteorological and natural wonders. Children love it, especially the interactive bits, even if none of the notices are in English. It's great fun for adults, too. Pick up a leaflet in English at the entrance, which shows the layout and helps you plan your route.

The Residenz Palace grand state rooms are another excellent place to head for when the weather forces you indoors (see page 66). The art gallery on the first floor is also worth spending time wandering round. And on a further artistic note, why not take more time to browse the Museum der Moderne contemporary art exhibitions up on Mönchsberg (see page 99). If it's raining, you won't be as distracted by the view as on a clear day.

End a rainy day with a traditional Austrian meal to warm and cheer you, followed by a wonderful classical concert.

⬥ *A fascinating display of natural history at Haus der Natur*

# On arrival

## TIME DIFFERENCE
Austria follows Central European Time (CET). During Daylight
Saving Time (late Mar–late Oct), the clocks are put ahead
one hour.

## ARRIVING
### By air
Wolfgang Amadeus Mozart Airport is very close to Salzburg's
centre, just off the Innsbrucker Bundesstrasse or A1 Westautobahn
motorway. You can get into town by car or taxi in 10–15 minutes.
A drop-off point and parking are available at the airport. You can
also get from the airport to Salzburg's main bus station, next to
the Hauptbahnhof (main railway station), on Bus 2 in 20 minutes.
It runs every 10 minutes in working hours (every 20 minutes in the
evening) Monday–Saturday, and every 30 minutes on Sundays.

### By rail
The Hauptbahnhof is located fairly centrally and has a
money exchange and kiosk. Right outside is the bus station.
ⓐ Südtirolerplatz

### By road
The left bank Old Town is mainly pedestrianised, as is much of
the right bank, so if you want to bring a car into Salzburg, you're
best to leave it in one of the large, centrally located car parks.
The Altstadt Garagen are within the rock of the Mönchsberg
mountain and from there you can walk to most sights within

## IF YOU GET LOST, TRY ...

**Excuse me, do you speak English?**
Entschuldigen Sie, sprechen Sie Englisch?
*Entshuldigen zee, shprekhen zee english?*

**Excuse me, is this the right way to the old town/the city centre/the tourist office/the station/the bus station?**
Entschuldigung, geht es hier zur Altstadt/zur Stadtmitte/zur Touristeninformation/zum Bahnhof/zum Busbahnhof?
*Entshuldeegoong, gayt es here tsoor altshtat/tsoor shtatmitter/zur Touristeninformasion/tsoom baanhof/tsoom busbaanhof?*

**Can you point to it on my map, please?**
Können Sie es mir bitte auf der Karte zeigen?
*Kernen see es meer bitter owf der kaarte tsygen?*

minutes. On the left bank Linzergasse Garagen is also very convenient. Alternatively, ask your hotel for the best place to park close to where you are staying; 24-hour parking usually costs around €15.

## FINDING YOUR FEET

Salzburg is a very safe city and there are no particular no-go areas. However, be aware of pickpockets, especially during the festival period and high season. If you want to get a real feel for the place, take a stroll around the small centre and along the

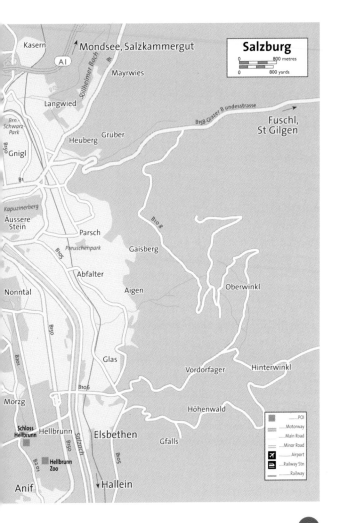

**FOR TECHNOS**

You can download a virtual guide onto your MP3 player or iPod® (🅦 www.pocketvox.com), and A1, a Vodafone partner, provides mobile phone English-language city guides to various sights (🅣 0664 664 664 🅦 www.a1.net).

river. Sit in a café or enjoy a cold beer to really appreciate the relaxed pace of life in this charming city.

## ORIENTATION

Salzburg's Old Town is enclosed by the two mountains Mönchsberg and Kapuzinerberg, with the River Salzach cutting it in half. The left bank is below the white fortress. Getreidegasse, the packed shopping street, runs through the centre of it. Mozartplatz, the main square where the composer's statue stands proud, is where you'll find the main tourist information office. The main traffic bridge between the two banks is Staatsbrücke. On the right bank the main streets are Linzer Gasse, Schwarzstrasse and Rainerstrasse, the latter of which leads to the central railway station. The whole old centre is easily walkable and you are unlikely to get lost.

Organised tours can give you an angle on the city you may not discover on your own. The following are recommended:

**Panorama Tours** 🅦 www.panoramatours.com

**Salzburg Guide Service** Offers one-hour tours starting daily at 12.15 from Information-Mozartplatz. 🅐 Linzergasse 22 🅣 0662 840 406 🅦 www.salzburg-guide.at

**Sightseeing Tours** Ⓦ www.salzburg-sightseeingtours.at

## GETTING AROUND

The bus system in Salzburg is excellent and efficient. Tickets are relatively cheap, but travel is free with a Salzburg Card. Tickets can be bought from the driver or at the ticket office in the bus terminal at the Hauptbahnhof, the main railway station with the bus station right next to it (Ⓐ Südtirolerplatz). Most buses leave from Mirabellplatz and the Hauptbahnhof on the right bank, or Hanuschplatz and Mozartsteg bridge on the left bank. You can pick up a free map from your hotel or any tourist information office, or visit Ⓦ www.stadtbus.at

Taxis can be called, pre-booked or found at ranks at the airport and main rail and bus station. Expect to pay around €13 from the airport to the centre and €5–8 from one side of the city centre to the other. A reliable 24-hour taxi firm is **Funk Taxi** (Ⓣ 0662 8111 or 0662 874 400).

### SALZBURG CARD

The best option for exploring the city is a Salzburg Card. This enables you to travel on public transport for free within the city and you also get a free single entry into all the attractions. Discounts on some tours, excursions and cultural events are also included. It's available for 24 hours, 48 hours or 72 hours, and children pay half price. Buy it from your hotel or tourist information office or purchase it by phone or email (Ⓣ 0662 8898 7454 Ⓔ cards@salzburg.info).

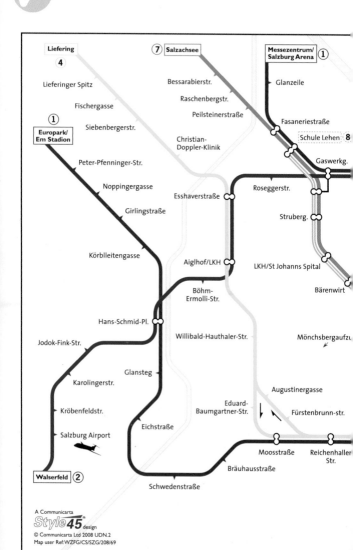

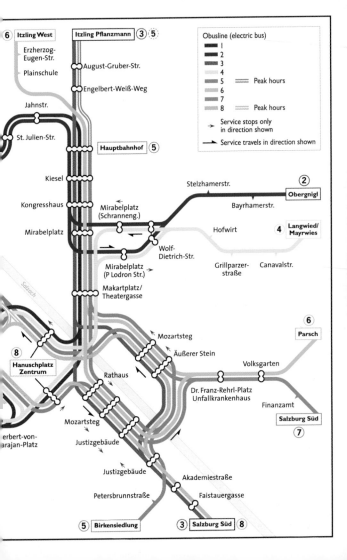

## PUBLIC TRANSPORT WITH A TWIST

Mönchsberg lift is the lift within the mountain. Leaving from Gstättengasse, it takes you directly up into the Museum der Moderne (Museum of Modern Art), where you can head outdoors for walks. The funicular railway to Festung Hohensalzburg is steep and swift and saves you a lot of legwork up lanes and steps. And, finally, there's the charming horse-drawn carriages (*Fiaker*), which start in Domplatz and cost around €35 for 25 minutes.

## CAR HIRE

This is advisable if you want to take trips out of the city and want more freedom than can be achieved with public transport. Just be aware that the city centre is a pedestrian zone and parking is expensive. Either pre-book to pick up your car at the airport, or get your hotel to arrange it for you. Check to see if your airline has special rates with a particular company.

**Avis** ❶ 0662 877 278 Ⓦ www.avis.com
**Budget** ❶ 0662 855 038 Ⓦ www.budget.com
**Europcar** ❶ 0662 871 616 Ⓦ www.europcar.com
**Hertz** ❶ 0662 876 674 Ⓦ www.hertz.com
**Sixt** ❶ 0662 856 051 Ⓦ www.e-sixt.com

● *The walkway leading to the restaurant at Hangar-7*

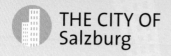

# Left bank Altstadt (Old Town)

The heart of the city contains some of Salzburg's oldest buildings and historical sights. It is a delight simply to wander around here, but if you want some true tourist value, hire a *Fiaker* (horse-drawn carriage). If you enter a church in time for a service you may experience some amazing classical music performances or organ recitals. And don't miss a look behind the scenes of the famous *Festspiele* concert halls.

A wonderfully unique sight is that of houses built into the rock of Mönchsberg. The sheer cliffs rise up behind the Old Town, forming an impressive backdrop, particularly dramatic in narrow Gstättengasse.

The Almkanal, an old medieval water system, still exists in working order and at various points you can see or hear water gushing and rushing down gullies. The water originates in Untersberg, a mountain south of Salzburg, and reaches the city via a series of underground tunnels.

When the city celebrates its founder on Rupertikirtag (St Rupert's Day Fair, 24 September), the normally sedate squares around the cathedral and Residenz Palace come alive with people, children's fairground rides, beer stands and craft stalls.

## SIGHTS & ATTRACTIONS

### Alte Hofapotheke

Still active, this ancient apothecary is full of the original wooden shelves and ceramic jars containing lotions and potions. **ⓐ** Alter Markt 6 **ⓘ** 0662 843 623 **ⓛ** 08.00–18.00 Mon–Fri, 08.00–12.00 Sat

**City river cruise**

Take a river boat trip along the Salzach, milky in colour from the limestone mixing with glacier water. Boats leave from the left bank pier below the Makartsteg footbridge. ⓦ www.salzburgschifffahrt.at ⓛ Apr–mid-Oct (starting times vary: phone ⓣ 0662 825 858 for details). Admission charge

**Dom (Cathedral)**

The baroque cathedral, majestic and vast, seats 10,000 people, which was the population when it was built in the 17th century.

● Take the weight off your feet with a horse and carriage ride

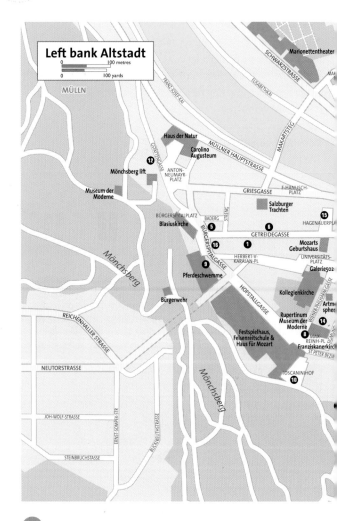

**Left bank Altstadt**

0 — 100 metres
0 — 100 yards

MÜLLN

MARIONETTENTHEATER
SCHWARZSTRASSE
ELISABETHKAI
FRANZ-JOSEF-KAI
MAKARTSTEG

Haus der Natur
Carolino Augusteum
MÜLLNER HAUPTSTRASSE
ANTON-NEUMAYR-PLATZ
GRIESGASSE
F. HANUSCH-PLATZ
GSTÄTTENGASSE
STEING.
BADERG.
Mönchsberg lift ❷
Museum der Moderne
BÜRGERSPITALPLATZ
Blasiuskirche ❺
Salzburger Trachten
❻
HAGENAUERPL
❶⑤
Mönchsberg
BÜRGERSPITALGASSE
GETREIDEGASSE
Mozarts Geburtshaus
HERBERT-V-KARAJAN-PL
Galerie502
UNIVERSITÄTS-PLATZ
Pferdeschwemme ❾
❶⑥
HOFSTALLGASSE
Kollegienkirche
Artmosphere
Bürgerwehr
Rupertinum Museum der Moderne ❽
WIENER-PHILHARMONIKER-GASSE
❶④
REICHENHALLER STRASSE
Festspielhaus, Felsenreitschule & Haus für Mozart
MAX-REINH-PL-ST
Franziskanerkirche
ST PETER BEZIR
NEUTORSTRASSE
Mönchsberg
TOSCANINIHOF
❶⓪
JOH-WOLF-STRASSE
ERNST-SOMPEK-STR
BÜRGL REUTH STRASSE
STEINBRUCHSTRASSE

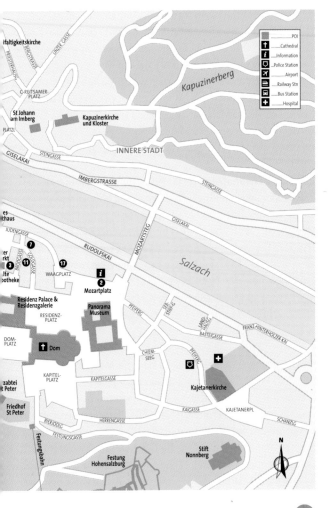

ifaltigkeitskirche

UNTERE GASSE

PRIESTERHAUSG

BERGSTRASSE

Kapuzinerberg

REITSAMER-PLATZ

St Johann
am Imberg

Kapuzinerkirche
und Kloster

PLATZL

GISELAKAI

STEINGASSE

INNERE STADT

IMBERGSTRASSE

STEINGASSE

es
thaus

JUDENGASSE

GISELAKAI

RUDOLFSKAI

MOZARTSTEG

Salzach

**7**

GOLDGASSE

CHIEMGASSE

er
rkt

**3**

**17**

WAAGPLATZ

lte
potheke

*i* **2**
Mozartplatz

Residenz Palace &
Residenzgalerie

RESIDENZ-
PLATZ

Panorama
Museum

PFEIFERG

DREIFALTIG.

LAND-
HAUSG

FRANZ-HINTERHOLZER-KAI

BASTEIGASSE

DOM-
PLATZ

**†** Dom

KAPITEL-
PLATZ

KAPITELGASSE

CHIEM-
SEEG

PFEIFERG

**◎**

**✛**

zabtei
t Peter

Friedhof
St Peter

BIERJODLG

HERRENGASSE

KAIGASSE

Kajetanerkirche

KAJETANERPL

SCHANZLG

Festungsbahn

FESTUNGSGASSE

Festung
Hohensalzburg

Stift
Nonnberg

N

| | POI |
|---|---|
| **†** | Cathedral |
| *i* | Information |
| **◎** | Police Station |
| **✈** | Airport |
| **⊟** | Railway Stn |
| **⊟** | Bus Station |
| **✛** | Hospital |

It boasts one of the largest mechanical organs in Europe, plus four others renovated recently, which Mozart played during his time as concert director here. Classical concerts form part of the 10.00 Sunday service. Arrive early for a seat. The acoustics are amazing. You can also see the basin where Mozart was baptised. ❷ Domplatz ⏱ 08.00–17.00 Mon–Sat, 13.00–17.00 Sun, Jan,Feb & Nov; 08.00–18.00 Mon–Sat, 13.00–18.00 Sun, Mar, Apr, Oct & Dec; 08.00–19.00 Mon–Sat, 13.00–19.00 Sun, May–July & Sept; 08.00–20.00 Mon–Sat, 13.00–20.00 Sun, Aug

### Erzabtei & Friedhof St Peter (St Peter Abbey & Cemetery)

The church and Benedictine monastery are both within the sanctified monks' territory, founded by St Rupert in 696. The view looking up to the fortress from the cemetery's arched entrance is awe-inspiring. You can visit the catacombs, which were revealed a few hundred years ago when part of the mountain crumbled away. The cemetery is full of old, intricately wrought iron crosses and is still used for graves today. ❸ St Peter Bezirk 1/2 ⏱ Catacombs: 10.30–17.00 Sun–Tues, May–Sept; 10.30–15.30 Wed & Thur, 10.30–16.00 Fri–Sun, Oct–Apr

### Festspielhaus, Felsenreitschule & Haus für Mozart

These three interlinked concert halls are where the *Festspiele* is staged. If you don't attend a concert, you can take a guided tour from the Festival Shop. In the Festspielhaus, marvel at the colourful frescoes in the marble foyer, its vast reception room and ceiling paintings, and the fireplace set into the mountain wall. The concert hall itself is one of Europe's largest and holds 2,179 guests (seat prices €50–500). The building was originally the stable block and indoor riding school of the prince-bishop's horses. Next door is the site of the Felsenreitschule, the summer riding school, where the prince's horses were trained in the warmer months. With its three arched galleries hewn out of the rock, it makes a stunning stage backdrop. You can also see here the archway filmed in *The Sound of Music*, through which the family fled from the Nazis. The Haus für Mozart, built in 2006, replaces what was known as the small festival hall. It has a state-of-the-art stage, acoustics and air-conditioned seating.

**Festival Shop & concert halls** ⓐ Hofstallgasse 1 ⓣ 0662 849 097 ⓦ www.salzburgfestival.at ⓛ 10.00–16.00

### Franziskanerkirche (Franciscan Church)

To get a picture of baroque in all its ornate and gilded glory, visit the Franciscan Church and be prepared to be awed by its gilt high altar and vaulted ceilings. ⓐ Sigmund-Haffner-Gasse ⓛ Services: 06.45, 09.00, 19.00 Mon–Sat, 09.00, 10.30, 19.00 Sun

### Getreidegasse

This street is rather like the main artery pumping visitors through the town. Lined with old-fashioned shops and a few modern boutiques dotted between Mozarts Geburtshaus (Mozart's birthplace) and the souvenir shops, the street provides a beautiful display of locally crafted iron signs.

### Mozarts Geburtshaus (Mozart's birthplace)

This is the small family house where Mozart was born and lived until he was 12. It has been pepped up with a stage-set display. See the tiny violin the young Mozart played. ⓐ Getreidegasse 9

**1** 0662 844 313 **W** www.mozarteum.at **L** 09.00–18.00 Sept–June, 09.00–19.00 July & Aug. Admission charge

### Pferdeschwemme (Horse Pond)

Also called Hofmarstallschwemme, this is a magnificent baroque pond decorated with frescoes of horses. The royal horses were washed here before returning to their stables next door.
**a** Herbert-von-Karajan-Platz

### Residenz Palace

Visit the 15 glorious state apartments full of rich red silk wall coverings, ancient tapestries, ceiling paintings and masterpieces of art. See how the former prince-archbishops resided in spacious splendour, amid mixed styles of Renaissance, rococo and classicism. **a** Residenzplatz 1 **1** 0662 8042 2690
**W** www.salzburg-burgen.at **L** 10.00–17.00. Admission charge

### Residenzplatz

The large square in front of the Residenz Palace has an elaborate baroque fountain and a Glockenspiel bell tower, which chimes at 07.00, 11.00 and 18.00, using a different melody every month.

## CULTURE

### Panorama Museum

This is a fascinating 360° picture of Salzburg painted in 1829 by Johann Michael Sattler. There are telescopes so you can get a closer look at the 130 sq m (426 sq ft) painting, and an interactive display compares it to today's view of the city. **a** Neue Residenz

⬥ *Mozart's birthplace in Getreidegasse is open to the public*

(Post Office entrance), Residenzplatz 9 🕿 0662 620 808 730
🕘 09.00–18.00 Fri–Wed, 09.00–20.00 Thur. Admission charge

### Private art galleries
Salzburg boasts some fine private art galleries that are open
free of charge to the public, including:

**Artmosphere** Housed in Palais Küenburg, this gallery specialises
in pop art. ⊜ Wiener-Philharmoniker-Gasse 3 🕿 0662 846 483
🌐 www.artmosphere.at 🕘 11.00–18.00 Tues–Fri, 10.00–15.00 Sat

**Galerie5020** Innovative contemporary art. ⊜ Sigmund-Haffner-
Gasse 12/1 🕿 0662 848 817 🌐 www.galerie5020.at 🕘 14.00–18.00
Tues–Fri, 10.00–13.00 Sat

### Residenzgalerie
A large gallery housing some magnificent works and interesting
temporary exhibitions on the second floor of the Residenz Palace.
Pleasant café and shop. ⊜ Residenzplatz 1 🕿 0662 8404 510
🌐 www.residenzgalerie.at 🕘 10.00–17.00 Tues–Sun ❶ With lots
of stairs and no lift, this venue is unsuitable for disabled visitors.
Admission charge

### Rupertinum Museum der Moderne
This is the central location of the Museum der Moderne, the other
being on top of Mönchsberg. See some interesting late 19th-
century black and white photos and paintings of the Salzburg
region, as well as a variety of contemporary art, including works
by Oskar Kokoschka. There are usually good temporary exhibitions

as well, and a nice café. ⓐ Wiener-Philharmoniker-Gasse 9
ⓣ 0662 842 220 ⓦ www.museumdermoderne.at ⓛ 10.00–18.00
Thur–Tues, 10.00–20.00 Wed. Admission charge

## RETAIL THERAPY

Within the stretch including Griesgasse, Getreidegasse and
Judengasse and off-shoots, you can find lots of well-known
international brand stores such as Benetton, Hugo Boss, Mango,
Zara, Esprit, H&M and Marc O'Polo. Goldgasse is a narrow alley
with jewellers and traditional shops selling stone beer mugs and
handmade leather goods. Alter Markt is the open marketplace
with several high-class fashion boutiques.

**Beurle** One of the classic shops for *Trachten* (traditional costumes),
it also has an exhibition and workshop. ⓐ Griesgasse 25
ⓣ 0662 843 119 ⓛ 09.00–18.00 Mon–Fri, 09.00–16.00 Sat

**Forsten Lechner** Boutique selling modern *Loden* and *Trachten*
clothing. Look out for the Luis Trenker label which gives the
traditional a modern twist. ⓐ Mozartplatz 4 ⓣ 0662 843 766
ⓦ www.salzburg-trachtenmode.at ⓛ 09.30–18.00 Mon–Fri,
09.30–17.00 Sat

**Höllrigl** Bookshop for books in English on Salzburg and local
recipes so you can recreate *Nockerl* or *Apfelstrudel* back home.
ⓐ Sigmund-Haffner-Gasse 10 ⓣ 0662 841 146 ⓛ 09.00–18.30
Mon–Fri, 09.00–18.00 Sat

**Käslöchl** A tiny shop selling a wonderful variety of cheeses, including goat's cheese, mature local alpine cheeses, beer cheese and Emmental. A great stop for picnic supplies or a take-home treat. ⓐ Hagenauerplatz 2 ⓣ 0662 844 100 ⓦ www.kasloechl.at ⓛ 09.00–18.00 Mon–Fri, 08.00–13.00 Sat

**Musikhaus Katholnigg** For classical and opera CDs or DVDs. ⓐ Sigmund-Haffner-Gasse 16 ⓣ 0662 841 451 ⓦ www.salzburg-cd.com ⓛ 09.30–12.30, 13.30–18.00 Mon–Fri, 09.30–16.00 Sat

**Spirituosen Sporer** For select Austrian wines, orange and Christmas punch, and homemade *Salzburg Vogelbeer Schnapps* (rowanberry schnapps). ⓐ Getreidegasse 39 ⓣ 0662 845 431 ⓦ www.sporer.at ⓛ 09.00–12.30, 14.30–19.00 Mon–Fri, 08.30–17.00 Sat

⬤ *Treat yourself to a Salzburger Nockerl*

**Stiftsbäckerei St Peter** The oldest bakery in town, originally set up by the monks. They produce fabulous *Holzofenbrot* (rye and sourdough bread baked in wood-ovens), which stays fresh for a week, so you can take a loaf home with you. The mill wheel is powered by the ancient water system. ⓐ Kapitelplatz 8 ⓣ 0662 847 898 ⓛ 07.00–17.30 Mon & Tues, Thur & Fri, 07.00–13.00 Sat

## TAKING A BREAK

**Balkan Grill £ ❶** A little booth serving Bosna, a hot-dog with a spicy pork sausage in four varieties. Originally Bulgarian, it's become an Austrian favourite too. ⓐ Getreidegasse 33 (in arcade) ⓣ 0662 841 483 ⓛ 11.00–19.00 Mon–Fri, 11.00–17.00 Sat, 16.00–20.00 Sun, July–Dec

**Café Demel £ ❷** An Austrian institution famous for its chocolate and fabulous catering services. The terrace is a prime spot for people-watching in summer. ⓐ Mozartplatz 2 ⓣ 0662 840 358 ⓦ www.demel.at ⓛ 09.00–19.00

**Café Konditorei Fürst £ ❸** The company who originally produced the chocolate Mozart Balls owns this café and the attached patisserie. ⓐ Alter Markt/Brodgasse 13 ⓣ 0662 8437 590 ⓦ www.original-mozartkugel.com ⓛ 08.00–20.00 Mon–Sat, 09.00–20.00 Sun

**Café Tomaselli £ ❹** Traditional coffee house established in 1705. *Mocca* and *Melange* are what to order, the menu won't say cappuccino or latte. Its patisserie boasts great cakes such as *Apfelstrudel* and *Gugelhupf* (ring cake). ⓐ Alter Markt 9 ⓘ 0662 844 488 ⓦ www.tomaselli.at ⓛ 07.00–20.30 Mon–Sat, 08.00–20.30 Sun

**Carpe Diem £ ❺** A stylish lounge café, named after the herbal health drink produced by Red Bull, who owns this place. Cute, tiny finger-food portions of cake are served with great coffees. ⓐ Getreidegasse 50 ⓘ 0662 8488 000 ⓦ www.carpediem.com ⓛ 08.30–00.00

**Eisgrotte £ ❻** For ice cream. ⓐ Getreidegasse 40 ⓘ 0662 843 157 ⓛ 09.00–23.00 (summer only)

**Saran Essbar £ ❼** A bar-café-restaurant that's affordable, cosy, quick and near the Getreidegasse shops. ⓐ Judengasse 10 ⓘ 0662 846 628 ⓛ 11.00–21.00

**Spoon £ ❽** Asian staples such as soups, curries and noodles provide tastes of the East in the Rupertinum. In a hurry? Take away a soup or curry in a bottle. ⓐ Wiener-Philharmoniker-Gasse 9 ⓘ 0662 841 00 ⓦ www.seehof-goldegg.com ⓛ 10.00–18.00 Mon, 10.00–01.00 Tues–Sat

## AFTER DARK

## RESTAURANTS
**Alt Salzburg £ ❾** A tiny restaurant with a cosy atmosphere, next to the Pferdeschwemme. ⓐ Bürgerspitalgasse 2 ⓘ 0662 841 476

ⓦ www.altsalzburg.at ⓛ 11.30–14.00, 18.00–00.00 Tues–Sat,
18.00–00.00 Mon

**Resch & Lieblich** £ ⓾ It means 'crisp and sweet', describing
the two varieties of *Most* (fruit wine), a typical Austrian drink
served here. The old restaurant is set back into the mountain.
ⓐ Toscaninihof 1A ⓣ 0662 843 675 ⓛ 11.00–21.00 June–mid-Jan;
11.00–21.00 Mon–Sat, mid-Jan–May

**Die Goldene Ente** ££ ⓫ The Golden Duck serves excellent
regional food and fabulous *Salzburger Nockerl* too. ⓐ Goldgasse 10
ⓣ 0662 8456 2230 ⓦ www.ente.at ⓛ 10.00–00.00

**Pan e Vin** ££ ⓬ A lovely Italian *trattoria* and restaurant tucked
into the Mönchsberg cliff. Good food and wines. See the cogs

⬤ *What about ordering Schnitzel with noodles?*

and workings of the Almkanal (Salzburg's underground water system) at the back of the restaurant. **ⓐ** Gstättengasse 1 **ⓣ** 0662 8446 6615 **ⓦ** www.panevin.at **ⓛ** 12.00–14.00, 18.00–23.00 Mon–Sat

**Stiftskeller St Peter ££ ⓭** Serves the best *Salzburger Nockerl* in town. This historic restaurant, professing to be the oldest in central Europe, offers elegant dining rooms, rustic rooms or cosy tables under the vaulted arches carved into the mountain. Excellent regional food. **ⓐ** St Peter Bezirk 1–4 **ⓣ** 0662 8412 680 **ⓦ** www.haslauer.at **ⓛ** 10.30–00.00

**Triangel ££ ⓮** Next to the Rupertinum Museum der Moderne near the Festspielhaus. Good quality food and vegetarian options. **ⓐ** Wiener-Philharmoniker-Gasse 7 **ⓣ** 0662 842 229 **ⓛ** 12.00–23.00 July, Aug & Dec; 12.00–23.00 Mon–Sat, Jan–June, mid-Sept–Nov

**Zum Eulenspiegel ££ ⓯** A tiny restaurant, often overlooked, tucked into the corner of a little square directly opposite Mozart's birthplace. Regional fare. **ⓐ** Hagenauerplatz 2, Getreidegasse **ⓣ** 0662 843 180 **ⓦ** www.zum-eulenspiegel.at **ⓛ** 10.00–00.00

**Blaue Gans £££ ⓰** Enjoy fine dining and excellent wines among the fun frescoes of the vaulted rooms in one of the city's oldest inns. **ⓐ** Getreidegasse 41–43 **ⓣ** 0662 8424 910 **ⓦ** www.blauegans.at **ⓛ** 12.00–00.00 Mon–Sat

**K&K £££ ⓱** This place enjoys a good reputation for traditional dishes. It has eight elegant old dining rooms, a summer terrace

out front and wonderful desserts. ⓐ Waagplatz 2 ⓣ 0662 842 156
ⓦ www.kkhotels.com ⓛ 11.00–14.00, 18.00–22.00

## BARS

**Humboldt Stubn** Offers a cool young vibe with Austrian food,
good vegetarian options and tapas. ⓐ Gstättengasse 4–6
ⓣ 0662 843 171 ⓦ www.humboldtstubn.at ⓛ 10.00–02.00

**Republic** The hippest café-bar-club in the city. They have live DJ
nights and special themed music nights such as fusion, Latin or
Brazilian. Great food and drinks too. Popular at any time of day
and buzzing at night. ⓐ Anton-Neumayr-Platz 2 ⓣ 0662 841 613
ⓦ www.republiccafe.at ⓛ 08.00–01.00 Sun–Thur, 08.00–04.00
Fri & Sat

## ARTS & ENTERTAINMENT

**Christmas Market** In Domplatz and Residenzplatz, this annual
event will get you into the festive spirit. Traditional wooden toys
and tree decorations, mulled wine and sweet Christmas treats,
all are here from the second week of November to Christmas Day.

**Mozart Dinner** Experience this at St Peter's Stiftskeller
restaurant. It's held in the ornate baroque ballroom where
dinner is complemented by performances of favourite arias
and duets from Mozart's operas. Tables sit up to 10, so you dine
with other visitors. It's expensive but worth it for high quality
food and music. ⓐ St Peter Bezirk 1–4 ⓣ 0662 8286 950
ⓦ www.mozartdinnerconcert.com ⓛ 20.00–22.30

# Right bank Altstadt (Old Town)

The Old Town on the right bank has a more open and less crowded feel than the left bank. The pretty Mirabell Gardens are the focal point and locals and visitors alike come here to relax.

Along the riverside is a well-used wide path for cyclists, joggers, rollerbladers and pedestrians. Three footbridges lead to the left bank: Mozartsteg, Makartsteg and Müllnersteg. The Staatsbrücke bridge in the centre takes traffic across as well and leads from the left bank town hall to the junction of Giselakai and Schwarzstrasse.

Kapuzinerberg (Capuchin Mountain) dominates the right bank. It provides another wonderful picturesque place to which

◆ *Hear musical masterpieces at the world-famous Mozarteum*

you can flee to escape the crowds and streets, and with a tranquil 16th-century monastery, beautiful woods and amazing views, it's a real haven.

Salzburg's main transport hub, the Hauptbahnhof (central train station) and the main bus terminal, is also located on this side of the river. Buses take you in all directions, whether you need to go to the airport, to the Stiegl brewery, out of town, to the foot of Gaisberg, or just across the river to Mozartplatz.

The right bank offers a more commercial and business side to the city, whereas the left bank is dominated by historical sights and tourism. You are more likely to find locals going about their day-to-day business here, especially on Thursdays at the busy market on Mirabellplatz around Andrä Church.

## SIGHTS & ATTRACTIONS

### Kapuzinerberg

Climb the 300 steps up to the Kapuzinerkloster (Capuchin monastery) and enjoy amazing views and walks in the woods. Stop for refreshments in the restaurant in a little castle on the peak. Take the gate in Linzergasse or the steps from Steingasse.

### Mozarteum

The Mozarteum University of Music and Dramatic Arts was renovated at a cost of €40 million. Its modern concrete cube, designed by Robert Rechanauer, sits at the edge of the Mirabell Gardens. You can go in and wander around the public areas to admire the architecture. There are also art exhibitions on the ground floor open to the public, and many concerts take place

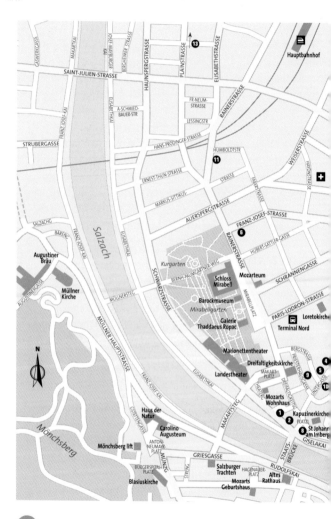

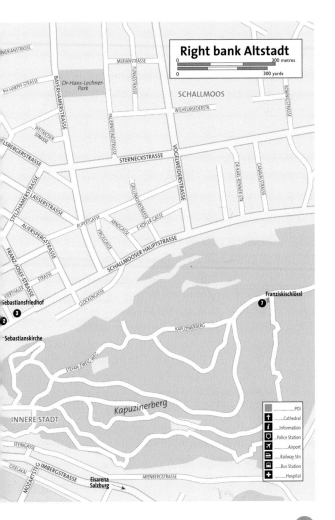

here in one of the four concert halls. ⓐ Mirabellplatz 1
ⓦ www.moz.ac.at

### Mozarts Wohnhaus (Mozart's Residence)

Mozart's family home is more interesting than his birthplace. He
composed most of his Salzburg works in this very house. Bombed
and partly destroyed in World War II, the house was reconstructed
and although the furniture pieces are of the period, they are not
the family's originals. There is a good permanent exhibition here
documenting the family's life and travels. ⓐ Makartplatz 8
ⓣ 0662 8742 2740 ⓦ www.mozarteum.at ⓛ 09.00–19.00 July
& Aug; 09.00–18.00 Sept–June. Admission charge

### Schloss Mirabell & Gardens (Mirabell Palace & Gardens)

The immaculate palace grounds are open free of charge to the
public. As you walk around, you'll notice some odd-looking dwarf
statues – a mysterious feature of Mirabell Gardens. The steps and
circular horse fountain here make an appearance in *The Sound of
Music*. The palace itself was built by Bishop Wolf Dietrich for his
mistress, Salome, in 1606. The Marmorsaal (Marble Hall) is the only
accessible room inside the buildings. You are welcome to have
a peek inside but viewing is not always possible as it is regularly
used for evening classical concerts, civil wedding ceremonies
and other events. ⓐ Mirabellplatz ⓣ 0662 8072 2334

### Sebastianskirche & Sebastiansfriedhof
### (Sebastian Church & Cemetery)

This large, smart church was rebuilt several times and so lost
a lot of its Gothic details. The cemetery has some tombstones

of famous Salzburgers such as Archbishop Wolf Dietrich, who had an elaborate mosaic mausoleum built in his own honour. The Mozart family grave (without Wolfgang Amadeus) is a more modest affair. ⓐ Linzergasse 41 ☎ 0662 875 208 ⏱ 09.00–16.00 winter; 09.00–18.30 summer

### Steingasse

A very old, narrow street with the original curfew gate and the house where Joseph Mohr – the composer of 'Silent Night', which is now sung in 260 languages – was born in 1792. The street is cool and quiet and gives you a glimpse into the past.

### Views

The best spot for taking photos is at the top of the steps in the Mirabell Gardens (remember the 'Do Re Me' scene in *The Sound of Music*?), looking up to the fortress. The alignment is perfect. A great view of the Old Town can be seen from Müllnersteg bridge. And, of course, you get a fabulous panorama from the Hotel Stein terrace café-bar, as well as from Kapuzinerberg.

## CULTURE

### Barockmuseum (Baroque Museum)

This museum is dedicated to baroque artists' maquettes and sketches. It houses the former private Rossacher collection, comprising around 200 preparatory works by some of the best baroque artists. Signs are all in German, but there is a leaflet available in English. There's also a Baroque Visions Slide Show with music at 11.00 and 15.00. ⓐ Orangery of the Mirabell Gardens,

Mirabellplatz 3 ☎ 0662 877 432 🕐 09.00–12.00, 14.00–17.00
Tues–Sat, 10.00–13.00 Sun. Admission charge

### Galerie Thaddaeus Ropac

Ropac is a revered gallery owner in art circles. You'll find good
temporary exhibitions of contemporary artists in this gallery
located in the Kast Villa in Mirabell Gardens. ⓐ Mirabellplatz 2
☎ 0662 881 393 Ⓦ www.ropac.net 🕐 10.00–18.00 Tues–Fri,
10.00–14.00 Sat

### Marionettentheater (Marionette Theatre)

This puppet theatre dates back to 1913. It is actually an adult venue
and not designed for children. Mozart's operas and other works
by Rossini, Strauss and Tchaikovsky are performed using the old
wooden puppets. Come and lose yourself in a miniature fantasy
world. All performances have English subtitles. Dress is as smart as
in a normal theatre. Check for performance details and times on
the website. In winter and spring the company goes on international
tour. ⓐ Schwarzstr. 24 ☎ 0662 872 406 Ⓦ www.marionetten.at
🕐 Performances usually 14.00 & 19.30 May–Sept; box office:
09.00–13.00 Mon–Sat & 2 hours before performances

## RETAIL THERAPY

Linzergasse is the right bank's main shopping street.
It has some traditional shops, restaurants and plenty of shoe
boutiques, and is far less touristy than Getreidegasse on the
other side. Dreifaltigkeitsgasse leads off towards Mirabellplatz
and offers small, interesting shops.

**Erlach** Traditional charcuterie and organic butcher's. It's a good place to stock up on provisions for a day trip or picnic. They sell salads in tubs, pizza slices, bread rolls, ham and sausages, chicken and schnitzel, plus a variety of drinks. ⓐ Linzergasse 3 ⓣ 0662 874 435 ⓛ 08.00–18.00 Mon–Fri, 08.00–12.00 Sat

⬥ *Wend your way down the charming, medieval Steingasse*

**Lanz Trachtenmoden** This was originally a sports shop run by two mountaineers, opened at the time the *Festspiele* first began. They stocked a few *Trachten* alongside the sports gear, and it was the former that really took off. Now they do big business with a workshop, several stores in Austria and even one in the USA. Enjoy browsing through the colourful array of *dirndl*, jackets, blouses and felt hats. ⓐ Schwarzstr. 4 ⓣ 0662 874 272 ⓦ www.lanztrachten.at ⓛ 09.00–18.00 Mon–Fri, 09.00–17.00 Sat

**Nagy & Söhne** A wonderful, family-run shop with a 125-year tradition, selling Hungarian honey gingerbread and homemade candles, both of which make nice gifts. ⓐ Linzergasse 32 ⓣ 0662 882 524 ⓦ www.nagy.at ⓛ 08.30–18.00 Mon–Fri, 09.00–13.00 Sat (09.00–16.00 first Sat of month)

**Schranne Market** Takes place all around the Andrä Church on Mirabellplatz on Thursday mornings. Here you'll find fresh local produce and traditional handicrafts. Grab a frankfurter as you stroll round this popular market. ⓛ 05.00–13.00 Thur

**Wein & Co Bar** Wine to taste and buy in the former home of Riedel, the manufacturer of the fine glassware which is still sold here. ⓐ Platzl 2 ⓣ 0662 876 925 ⓦ www.weinco.at ⓛ 10.00–23.00

## TAKING A BREAK

**Café Bazar £ ①** One of Salzburg's traditional coffee houses with a historical background, and a favourite with literary types and actors. Enjoy the fine wooden panelling in winter and the sunny terrace with views over the river in summer. Great breakfasts served all day. ⓐ Schwarzstr. 3 ❶ 0662 874 278 ⓦ www.cafe-bazar.at ⓛ 07.30–23.00 Mon–Sat, 09.00–18.00 Sun

**Café Sacher £ ❷** The Hotel Sacher's famous café where you can sample their very rich chocolate cake, still handmade to the original recipe. In summer relax under the chestnut trees and watch joggers, cyclists and pedestrians pass along the river's edge. ⓐ Schwarzstr. 5–7 ❶ 0662 889 770 ⓛ 07.30–00.00

**Capp&ccino £ ❸** This modern coffee bar serves great coffees. Also light, bistro-style food and other drinks. ⓐ Linzergasse 39 ❶ 0662 875 545 ⓦ www.cappuccino-salzburg.at ⓛ 08.00–22.00

**Fuchshofer £ ❹** Yet another cake shop and bakery with a café, perfect for a pit stop while shopping. It has modern flair and fabulous homemade nut and carrot bread. ⓐ Linzergasse 13 ❶ 0676 7285 266 ⓛ 09.00–19.00

**Gablerbräu £ ❺** A traditional little café-restaurant which offers light lunches of pasta dishes, salads and soups. ⓐ Linzergasse 9 ❶ 0662 889 65 ⓦ www.gablerbrau.com ⓛ 11.00–00.00

**Wernbacher £ ❻** A great 50s-style café serving wonderful breakfasts and Austrian cuisine, plus a reasonable midday fixed menu. Relaxed atmosphere. ⓐ Franz-Josef-Str. 5 ❶ 0662 881 099 ⓦ www.cafewernbacher.at ⓛ 09.00–00.00 Mon–Fri, 09.00–20.00 Sat

**Wirtshaus im Franziskischlössl £ ❼** Typical regional food all year round with some speciality meat dishes. Lovely garden at 634 m (2,080 ft). ⓐ Kapuzinerberg 9 ❶ 0662 872 595 ❷ 10.00–19.00 June–Sept; 10.00–17.00 Oct–May

## AFTER DARK

### RESTAURANTS
**Steinterrasse £ ❽** A sophisticated, very modern lounge with great wines and an affordable pan-Mediterranean menu. The view is stunning, offering a whole panorama across the city and up Kapuzinerberg. A trendy place to see and be seen. ⓐ Giselakai 3–5 ❶ 0662 882 070 ⓦ www.steinterrasse.at ❷ 09.00–00.00

**Zum fidelen Affen £ ❾** This pub-type venue is affordable, fun and popular with students. The menu is a mix of rustic regional dishes. ⓐ Priesterhausgasse 8 ❶ 0662 877 361 ❷ 17.00–00.00 Mon–Sat

**Stadtkrug ££ ❿** A traditional restaurant in the hotel of the same name. Local specialities are on the menu here. ⓐ Linzergasse 20 ❶ 0662 873 545 ⓦ www.stadtkrug.at ❷ 12.00–14.30, 18.00–00.00

**Stieglbräu ££ ⓫** Run by the famous Salzburger brewery, the restaurant in their hotel serves traditional Austrian food and, of course, beer. Enjoy the beer garden in summer. ⓐ Rainerstr. 14 ❶ 0662 877 694 ⓦ www.imlauer.com ❷ 11.00–00.00

**Weinschmecker ££ ⓬** Tucked away in Bruderhof, a courtyard between Linzergasse and the Loretokirche, is a fun and popular wine bar-cum-restaurant. It has a young, contemporary feel and offers excellent regional and international wines as well as light meals. ⓐ Bruderhof, Linzergasse 39 ⓣ 0664 4058 298 ⓛ 18.00–late Tues–Thur, 15.00–late Fri & Sat

**Plainlinde £££** ⓭ A fabulous gourmet restaurant 15 minutes from the city centre but worth the taxi fare there and back. Run by two young experts, one in the kitchen and the other in the wine trade. ⓐ Plainbergweg 30, Bergheim ⓣ 0662 458 557

⬤ *Stop for 'tea – a drink with jam and bread'?*

ⓦ www.plainlinde.at ⓛ 12.00–14.00, 19.00–21.00 Wed–Sun
ⓘ Booking essential

## BARS

**Alter Fuchs** A traditional and cosy *Stadtwirtshaus* (local pub),
also serving hearty meals. ⓐ Linzergasse 47 ⓣ 0662 882 022
ⓛ 12.00–00.00

**Bazillus Bar & Lounge** Looking out over the river and across at
the Old Town, you can relax here with a drink and bar snacks
such as salads and tapas. The wonderful terrace is open in the
warmer months. ⓐ Imbergstr. 2A ⓣ 0662 871 631 ⓛ 14.00–02.00
Mon–Thur, 18.00–04.00 Fri–Sun ⓝ Bus: 3, 5, 6, 7, 8, 10, 25, 26

**Fridrich** A lovely, cosy little wine bar in the old Steingasse
with a good selection of Austrian wines. ⓐ Steingasse 15
ⓣ 0662 876 218 (after 17.00) ⓛ 18.00–01.00 Thur–Tues

**Saitensprung** This wine bar in the heart of the old right bank
is popular with young Salzburgers. It's cut into the rock of
Kapuzinerberg. Good for drinks and close to the cinema.
The name means 'snapped guitar string'. ⓐ Steingasse 11
ⓣ 0662 881 377 ⓛ 21.00–04.00 Sun–Wed, 21.00–05.00 Thur–Sat

**Sketch Bar** Within the Bristol Hotel, this bar lounge is a smart
destination for happy-hour drinks, aperitifs and cocktails. Also
pre-theatre meals and business lunches. ⓐ Makartplatz 4
ⓣ 0662 873 557 ⓦ www.bristol-salzburg.at ⓛ 11.00–00.00

**Steinlechner** Another hip hangout located near the ice rink. It has a good bar and food plus a nice garden for summer. ⓐ Aignerstr. 4–6 ⓣ 0662 633 633 ⓦ www.steinlechnersbg.at ⓛ 10.00–01.00 Sun–Wed, 10.00–03.00 Thur–Sat ⓝ Bus: 7

**Steinterrasse** The hotspot to meet up for drinks on the seventh floor of Hotel Stein. The location is perfect, right on the river overlooking the whole city and the mountain looming behind. Glistening mosaic-tiled bars, curves and stylish seating make you feel like you've walked into an interior décor magazine. A good choice of wines, beers and other drinks. ⓐ Giselakai 3–5 ⓣ 0662 874 346 ⓦ www.steinterrasse.at ⓛ 09.00–00.00 Sun–Thur, 09.00–01.00 Fri & Sat

## ARTS & ENTERTAINMENT

**Das Kino** This riverside cinema often shows films in the original language with German subtitles, so check listings or the free poster-size folded programme, *Kultplan*. It covers the best of Salzburg's arts programme each month and can be picked up from the cinema foyer. ⓐ Giselakai 11 ⓣ 0662 873 100 ⓦ www.daskino.at ⓛ Programme varies – check website for details

**Eisarena Salzburg** You can hire skates at this ice skating arena and use the 3,600 sq m (11,800 sq ft) rink as long as there isn't an ice-hockey match going on. Catch a bus out to the Volksgarten Park to get there. ⓐ Hermann-Bahr-Promenade 2 ⓣ 0662 623 411 4373 ⓛ 10.00–16.15 summer; 19.45–21.30 Mon, Wed, Thur & Sat, winter ⓝ Bus: 6, 7, 20. Admission charge

**Jazzit** This music club has some great jazz concerts and a free jam session on Tuesdays in the bar. Look online for the schedule and prices. ⓐ Elisabethstr. 11 ⓣ 0662 883 264 ⓦ www.jazzit.at ⓛ 18.00–late Mon–Sat

**Kleines Theater** Check listings or the online programme for possible music concerts. The plays are all in German. ⓐ Schallmooser Hauptstr. 50 ⓣ 0662 872 154 ⓦ www.kleinestheater.at ⓛ Programme varies – check website for details ⓝ Bus: 4

**Landestheater** A lovely old theatre with traditional décor and classic performances. Plays are all in German, and operas are also performed here. ⓐ Schwarzstr. 22 ⓣ 0662 8715 120 ⓦ www.salzburger-landestheater.at ⓛ Programme varies – check website for details

**Literaturhaus** Salzburg's 'Literature House' hosts a very active literary circle which organises regular readings and meetings. Unfortunately for English-speakers, the majority of events are in German. Check the online programme or visit for information on local authors. ⓐ Strubergasse 23 ⓣ 0662 422 411 ⓦ www.literaturhaus-salzburg.at ⓛ Programme varies – check website for details

**Rock House** This blue venue hosts gigs by national and international bands, mainly alternative, rock and electro-pop, and cool DJs. It's a little way out of the centre but you can get a bus. ⓐ Schallmooser Hauptstr. 46 ⓣ 0662 884 914 ⓦ www.rockhouse.at ⓛ Programme varies – check website for details ⓝ Bus: 4

**Salzburger Schlosskonzerte** Daily classical concerts are held in the beautiful baroque Marble Hall of Schloss Mirabell. This tradition started back in 1954. You can book a pre-event dinner at the Sheraton hotel's Mirabell restaurant. ⓐ Mirabellplatz 4 ⓘ 0662 848 586 ⓦ www.salzburger-schlosskonzerte.at ⓛ Programme varies – check website for details. Admission charge

⬥ *The exquisite Marble Hall in the Mirabell Palace*

# Mönchsberg, Nonnberg & beyond

As a real contrast to the throngs of tourists in the Getreidegasse and the in-your-face Mozart marketing all over the city, the natural beauty to be found within minutes of the town centre is a haven of space and tranquillity. Once you've had your fill of culture and the buzz of the city, escape to Mönchsberg to clear your mind and get some R&R. You can't beat the fresh air, aesthetic panorama, peace and quiet, and colours of the woods' changing seasons. The magnificent fortress, Festung Hohensalzburg, watches over the city from on high. Its light-coloured stone is striking in bright sunlight.

The mountain is 3 km (2 miles) long and paths weave their way through the shady woods, offering plenty of well-positioned benches en route. Numerous lookout points provide fascinating views over the city, each one different. There is no shortage of places to have refreshments, whether you are in the fortress, the art museum, a little kiosk in the middle of the woods, or the ancient beer gardens at either end of the mountain.

At the far end of Mönchsberg is Nonnberg (Nuns' Mountain), where a large church and convent overlook the part of the city called Nonntal (Nuns' Valley). This area is much quieter and more residential than the old centre. A few interesting traditional craft shops can be found in the lanes, as well as some good places to eat.

## SIGHTS & ATTRACTIONS

### Bürgerwehr (Fortification)

The impressive fortification walls are still standing, about half way along Mönchsberg on the town side. Take a look at the reconstruction on the notice board to see where the rest of the walls were. Dating back to the pre-artillery 13th century, it defended Mönchsberg and the city below against attack. The straight walls and five towers, built with little stones, provided a strong strategic defence. It became obsolete when explosives were invented.

## Festung Hohensalzburg (Hohensalzburg Fortress)

The fortress on top of Mönchsberg is a must for any visitor. You can look up at it from every point in the Old Town. Reach the landmark by foot (via a strenuously steep footpath and steps) or take the easy option by catching the funicular. The stunning, white-stone medieval fortress takes you back through more than 900 years of history. You can even see some Roman ruins and the uncovered part of the peak where the first settlers came. Follow the signs which lead you around the courtyards, towers and inner rooms which hold museums and the torture chamber. The state rooms are magnificent, especially the Gold Chamber with its gold buttons (representing the stars) on blue and red wooden ceilings and walls. There's even a very primitive toilet. A lovely video (Multivision Show) runs in one room, showing the fortress from all angles and in all weathers, as well as the inner workings which you wouldn't normally see. The armoury has a rather eerie battle-inspired display where the weapons and armour seem to take on a life of their own. Then there's the torture instrument room, where you can either laugh or be suitably appalled at the grotesque ancient punishments, masks of disgrace and chastity belt. See the unearthed treasure of gold coins and some very old beer tankards and bowls. There

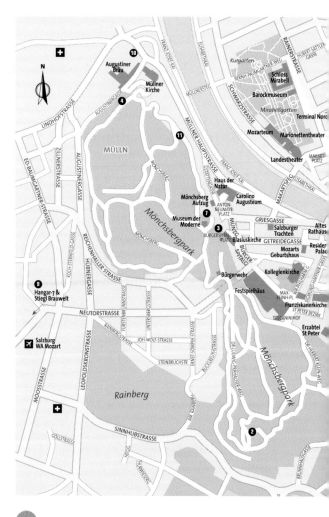

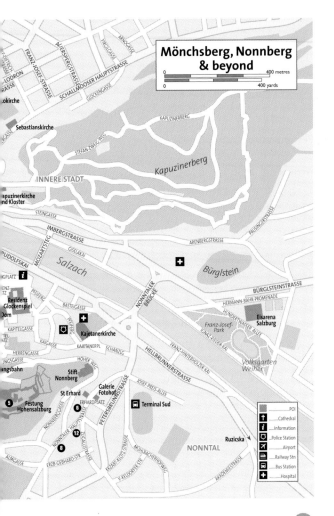

is a little puppet museum, too, where you can see the wooden puppets close up. Outdoors you can climb one of the lookout towers, enjoy the open spaces of the vast courtyards or visit the various cafés and terraces, all with stunning views. Audioguides are available. ❶ 0662 8424 3011 Ⓦ www.salzburg-burgen.at ◐ 09.30–17.00 Oct–Apr; 09.00–19.00 May–Sept. Admission charge

### Festungsbahn (Fortress Train)

The swift funicular transport up to the fortress leaves every 10 minutes, and runs after hours when fortress concerts are on. ⓐ Festungsgasse 4 ❶ 0662 8884 9750 Ⓦ www.salzburg-ag.at ◐ 09.00–22.00 May–Aug; 09.00–21.00 Sept; 09.00–17.00 Oct–Apr. Admission charge

### Mönchsberg Aufzug (Mönchsberg Lift)

The lift up the mountain is accessible until the early hours. ⓐ Gstättengasse 13 ❶ 0662 8884 9750 Ⓦ www.salzburg-ag.at ◐ 08.00–19.00 Thur–Tues, 08.00–21.00 Wed, May, June & Sept; 08.00–01.00 July & Aug; 08.00–19.00 Thur–Tues, 08.30–21.00 Wed, Oct–Apr. Small admission charge, but free with the Salzburg card

### Mönchsberg Woods

Put on your walking shoes and make the most of the lovely deciduous woods full of beech and rowan trees. The paths cover the 3 km (2 mile) length of the mountain up at a height of over 500 m (1,640 ft). There's plenty to do, even for children, from the art gallery to the fortress, woods, cafés and old fortification walls. You could spend all day up here. It's a protected area, so no camping and no rubbish allowed.

## Stiegl Brauwelt

Visit the city's famous brewery and its large exhibition focusing on the wonderful world of beer. You may even see the dappled horses, which draw the old-fashioned beer trailers, being trained on the field in front of the huge brewery. The exhibition is well executed and takes you through the whole process from raw ingredients and fermenting to brewing, bottling and marketing. Included in the entry fee are two beers (or non-alcoholic drinks if you prefer) and a *Brezel* in the brewery's pub at the end of the tour. You can easily spend a full two hours here. It's accessible by bus, and they have ample parking as well. ⓐ Bräuhausstr. 9 ❶ 0662 8387 1492 ⓦ www.brauwelt.at ⓛ 10.00–17.00 Sept–June; 10.00–19.00 July & Aug ⓝ Bus: 1. Admission charge

## Stift Nonnberg (Nonnberg Convent)

At the end of Mönchsberg farthest from the Museum der Moderne is the Nonnberg Convent. The Benedictine convent is the oldest in German-speaking Europe, established by St Rupert in 700. The church was erected later. The late-Gothic doors and frescoes are particularly lovely, and the area exudes monastic peace and calm. ⓛ 07.00–dusk

## Views

Mönchsberg is the highest level of the city, so there are naturally many places up there where you can get exceptional views of Salzburg and the surrounding area. The fortress and M32 terrace are particularly magic spots, conducive to sitting for hours and enjoying the views below. From Nonnberg you look out over the valley south of the city, and from the highest point of the mountain, Richterhöhe, you get a wide perspective over the Max Glan area out towards the airport. Wherever you wander, you won't be short of photo opportunities.

## CULTURE

### Galerie Fotohof

A renowned gallery in Nonntal supporting contemporary photographers. It displays work by renowned international stars such as Nan Goldin, Bernd and Hilla Becher, as well as local talent. The gallery hosts about ten exhibitions a year.
ⓐ Erhardplatz 3 ⓣ 0662 849 296 ⓦ www.fotohof.at
ⓛ 15.00–19.00 Mon–Fri, 10.00–13.00 Sat

⬥ *Austrian and international art at Museum der Moderne*

### Museum der Moderne (Museum of Modern Art)

Salzburg's stylish and contemporary art museum showcases 20th-century avant-garde large-scale solo exhibits from artists such as Shirin Neshat, Erwin Wurm, William Kentridge and Markus Raetz. If you want your visit to coincide with an opening preview, check the website. ⓐ Mönchsberg 32 ⓣ 0662 842 220 403 ⓦ www.museumdermoderne.at ⓛ 10.00–18.00 Tues & Thur–Sun, 10.00–20.00 Wed. Admission charge

### Numbers in the Woods

Italian artist Mario Merz was commissioned in 2003 by the Salzburg Foundation to create an installation up on Mönchsberg. His series of numbers light up in neon blue at night and can be seen from afar. Close to one of the lookout points near the Museum der Moderne, the numbers are hidden among trees and bushes, linked on arcs of wire. The mysterious numbers follow a formula written by a medieval Italian mathematician.

### Ruzicska

This relatively new gallery in Nonntal has become a top art address in Salzburg. ⓐ Faistauergasse 12 ⓣ 0662 630 360 ⓦ www.ruzicska.com ⓛ 10.00–18.00 Tues–Fri, 10.00–14.00 Sat

## RETAIL THERAPY

Nonntaler Hauptstrasse offers the only retail in this area, whose main draw is, of course, the natural surroundings. You can learn about traditional craftsmanship and find handmade clothing and jewellery by local designers. You won't find any commercial shops here.

**Festung Christmas Market** Within the courtyard of the Festung Hohensalzburg you are treated to a special festive delight in the form of a little Christmas market. Source some lovely gifts and trinkets here. 🕐 10.00–18.00 every weekend during Advent

**Gwandhaus** A great way to immerse yourself in the world of *Trachten* (traditional costume). In the south of the city on the way out towards Hellbrunn, this attractive former hotel and estate now houses the Gössl company's showroom and little museum. You need to drive or take a bus, but there's an inviting café-restaurant here if you need sustenance. This is where the locals come for something special, such as tailor-made dresses and suits for weddings. The pretty hall is used for folk music concerts and weddings. ⓐ Morzger Str. 31 ☎ 0662 469 660 ⓦ www.gwandhaus.com 🕐 10.00–20.00 ⓝ Bus: 25

**Lederhosen Karner** Watch the masters at work in this little shop and workshop as they make, decorate and repair the traditional alpine leather shorts. ⓐ Nonntaler Hauptstr. 21 ☎ 0662 840 112 ⓦ www.lederhosen-karner.com 🕐 08.30–12.00, 14.00–18.00 Mon–Fri

**Museum der Moderne** As you would expect, the shop in the Museum of Modern Art sells prints, books and knick-knacks related to contemporary art. ⓐ Mönchsberg 32 ☎ 0662 842 220 403 ⓦ www.museumdermoderne.at 🕐 10.00–18.00 Tues & Thur–Sun, 10.00–20.00 Wed

## TAKING A BREAK

**Burgschenke £ ❶** Within the fortress grounds, this café
offers great views and a variety of light meals, coffee and
cakes. ⓐ Mönchsberg 34 ❶ 0662 844 975 ⓦ www.ritteressen-
salzburg.at ⓛ 10.00–18.00

**Kiosk café £ ❷** In the middle of Mönchsberg woods you can have
drinks, snacks, coffees and toasted sandwiches. ⓐ Mönchsberg
ⓛ Noon–dusk Tues–Sun

**Stadtalm £ ❸** A delightful café and little restaurant offering
simple fare with fantastic views from the garden terrace.
ⓐ Naturfreundehaus am Mönchsberg ❶ 0662 841 729
ⓦ www.diestadtalm.at ⓛ 10.00–18.00 Apr & Oct; 10.00–23.00
May–Sept

**Magazin ££ ❹** This is a modern restaurant, 'vinothek' and shop.
Great for lunches. Have a browse in the wine shop before you leave.
ⓐ Augustinergasse 13 ❶ 0662 841 584 ⓦ www.magazin.co.at
ⓛ 10.00–00.00 Tues–Sat

**Restaurant zur Festung Hohensalzburg ££ ❺** Dine like knights
and ladies in the fortress overlooking the city. A slap-up meal or
simpler fare; it's your choice. ⓐ Mönchsberg 34 ❶ 0662 841 780
ⓦ www.festungsrestaurant.at ⓛ 09.00–18.00 May;
09.00–19.00 July–Sept

## AFTER DARK

### RESTAURANTS

**Lemon Chilli £ ❻** A fun and colourful cantina and Mexican bar with space indoors and out. ⓐ Nonntaler Hauptstr. 24 ❶ 0662 842 558 Ⓦ www.lemonchilli.at ⓛ 11.00–14.30, 17.00–00.30

**M32 ££ ❼** The fabulous restaurant designed by Matteo Thun serves Austro-Mediterranean cuisine. Enjoy the views and huge terrace. ⓐ Mönchsberg 32 ❶ 0662 841 000 Ⓦ www.m32.at ⓛ 09.00–01.00 Tues–Sat, 09.00–18.00 Sun

**Prosecco ££ ❽** An Italian restaurant with a lovely garden you can sit in when the weather's warm. ⓐ Nonntaler Hauptstr. 55 ❶ 0662 834 017 ⓛ 11.30–14.30, 18.00–00.00 Mon–Fri, 18.00–00.00 Sat & Sun

**Ikarus ££–£££ ❾** Chef Andres Madrigal Garcia serves up his own takes on superstar chefs' signature dishes in amazing modern surroundings. The menu changes on a regular basis. ⓐ Wilhelm-Spazier-Str. 7A ❶ 0662 219 777 Ⓦ www.hangar-7.com ⓛ 12.00–14.00, 18.30–22.00

**Esszimmer £££ ❿** A sleek restaurant with tasteful, colourful décor and four set menus which you can mix and match. ⓐ Müllner Hauptstr. 33 ❶ 0662 870 899 Ⓦ www.esszimmer.com ⓛ 12.00–14.00, 18.30–01.00 Tues–Sat Ⓝ Bus: 7, 8, 10, 16, 18, 24, 27

**Paris Lodron £££** ⓫ A pricey restaurant in the Hotel Schloss Mönchstein. Romantic and high quality food and wines. A fabulous modern glass structure complements the old castle, and views of the woods are thrown in as well. ⓐ Mönchsbergpark 26 ⓣ 0662 8485 550 ⓦ www.monchstein.at ⓛ 12.00–14.00, 18.00–21.30

**Purzelbaum £££** ⓬ A cosy little bistro restaurant with a good reputation located near St Erhard Church in Nonntal. Art nouveau décor. ⓐ Zugallistr. 7 ⓣ 0662 848 8433 ⓦ www.purzelbaum.at ⓛ 12.00–14.00, 18.00–23.00 Tues–Sat

## BARS
**Augustinerbräu Kloster Mülln** Beer garden of the monks. Take your own food or buy from the butcher or fishmonger in the

⬥ *Lavish dining at the Salzburg fortress*

hall. Enjoy cold, cloudy beer in stone mugs cooled under the fountain. ⓐ Lindhofstr. 7 ⓣ 0662 431 246 ⓛ 15.00–23.00 Mon–Fri, 15.00–22.30 Sat & Sun

**Mayday** The cool bar within Hangar-7, near the airport. Great drinks, atmosphere and fun interactive games integrated into the bar. ⓐ Wilhelm-Spazier-Str. 7A ⓣ 0662 219 777 ⓦ www.hangar-7.com ⓛ 17.30–late

**Stieglkeller** This beer garden is a must for the view over the city alone. Climb the 60 steps to sample beer from Salzburg's oldest brewery, established in 1492. ⓐ Festungsgasse 10 ⓣ 0662 842 681 ⓦ www.imlauer.com ⓛ 11.00–22.30

## ARTS & ENTERTAINMENT
**ARGEKultur** The alternative venue for performing arts. ⓐ Josef-Preis-Allee 16 ⓣ 0662 848 784 ⓦ www.argekultur.at ⓛ Office: 09.00–14.00; infopoint: 17.00–19.00

**Salzburger Festungskonzerte** A classical concert in one of the most stunning fortresses in Europe... with or without the four-course dinner in the fortress restaurant, it will be a memorable experience. Enjoy 'Eine kleine Nachtmusik' and a plethora of other offerings by Mozart, Schubert, Brahms or Beethoven. ⓐ Box office, Adlgasser Weg 22 ⓣ 0662 825 858 ⓦ www.mozartfestival.at ⓛ 20.00 or 20.30 May–Oct

ⓞ *A proud unicorn guards Hellbrunn Palace*

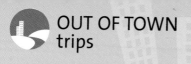

# Hellbrunn

Escape the city for a day and head south to Hellbrunn, 5 km
(3 miles) from Salzburg's centre. Schloss Hellbrunn (Hellbrunn
Palace) is the main attraction, built as a summer residence for
Markus Sittikus, one of the prince-archbishops. He came here for
amusement and most of the surrounding sights and attractions
offer just that. You can spend a day or longer exploring the area.
It is all easily accessible on the bus route out of town, and if
you carry on beyond Hellbrunn, you will reach the mysterious
Untersberg, home to many a legend. There's a cable car which
takes you up the mountain and into a world of alpine pastures,
hiking and paragliding.

## GETTING THERE

Hellbrunn is a popular destination with cyclists, as the bike route
takes you along the river before leading you down a pretty, tree-
lined avenue into the vast grounds and park at Hellbrunn. Hire a
bike in the city (see page 35) and you'll be in Hellbrunn in half an
hour. Alternatively, you can hop on the river boat from Makartsteg
pier. The boat drops you at the point near Salzburg Süd (south)
and you can just walk through to Schloss Hellbrunn. Drivers can
take the Hellbrunner Strasse B150 on the left bank out of town
and then drive along the Morzger Strasse through the village of
Morzg and on to Hellbrunn, where there's ample parking. Bus 25
leaves from the main bus station or from Mozartsteg bridge and
takes 20 minutes to get to Hellbrunn. The bus drives through the
villages of Morzg, Hellbrunn and Anif and under the E55 motorway

## SIGHTS & ATTRACTIONS

### Hellbrunnerallee

Along the beautiful tree-lined avenue leading up to Schloss
Hellbrunn are several privately owned castles and manor
houses, many being the summer escapes for the rich bishops
and former rulers of Salzburg. Keep your eyes open for Schloss
Freisaal (built in 1392), Frohnburg (1672), Schloss Emsburg (1618)
and Schloss Emslieb (1618), all visible from the road.

△ *Another top attraction: Hellbrunn Palace and gardens*

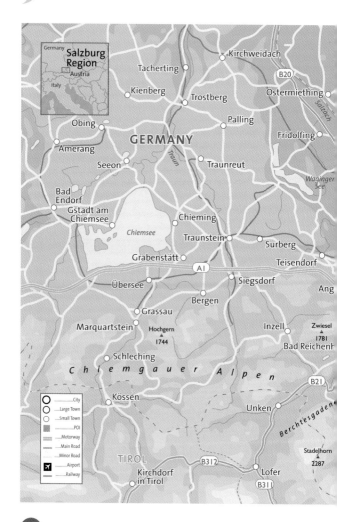

### Hellbrunn Park

The vast open space and beautifully kept parkland belonging to Schloss Hellbrunn is free to visit, and in fine weather you'll see plenty of locals heading out here to stroll, let the kids play in the adventure playground, picnic, cycle, rollerblade or jog. There are seats in the sun, lawns, shady spots, a protected stretch of old oak trees, and some pieces of modern art dotted around the gardens. You can even see the pavilion used in the filming of the romantic scene 'I am sixteen going on seventeen...' in *The Sound of Music*. Don't miss a walk through the beautiful beech woods to see the fabulous Stone Theatre, hewn out of the rocks.
🕐 06.30–17.00 Jan, Feb, Nov & Dec; 06.30–18.00 Mar & Oct; 06.00–21.00 Apr–Sept

### Salzburg Zoo

Wedged between the walls of Schloss Hellbrunn and the hill, this park has animals from all over the world, divided by continent. It takes about an hour and a half to walk around the whole area. There is a shop, restaurant, snack stands and public toilets, plus free parking. From gibbons to wild cats, red pandas to rhinos, and flamingos to chamois, you'll find something here to charm everyone in the family. ⓐ Anifer Landesstr. 1 ⓣ 0662 8201 760 ⓦ www.salzburg-zoo.at 🕐 09.00–18.00

### Schloss Hellbrunn (Hellbrunn Palace)

This ochre yellow palace set in beautiful parkland was built by Prince Markus Sittikus as his summer residence in 1613. He never actually lived here, but held regular parties and hunts. Ponds with sturgeon and trout, statues, immaculate landscaped gardens and flowerbeds plus beech woods up on the hill make up the grounds. The various rooms around the palace all have themed names corresponding to the paintings or decoration, such as Fish Room or Chinese Room. Some fine old paintings of nature and animals are also to be seen about the place. Keep an eye open particularly for the octagonal music room, the Italian frescoes in the festival hall, and Markus Sittikus's ubiquitous coat of arms (a prancing goat and lion). ⓐ Fürstenweg 37 ⓣ 0662 8203 720 ⓦ www.hellbrunn.at ⓛ 09.00–17.30 May, June & Sept; 09.00–22.00 July & Aug. Admission charge includes audioguide

◯ The Trick Fountains are great fun in the Hellbrunn gardens

### Untersberg

This mountain is 1,852 m (6,080 ft) high. Legend has it that Charlemagne is still sleeping in the mountain, and he will wake when he is most needed, and when the ravens no longer fly around the top of the mountain. Fantastic views, walks, alpine pastures, ice caves and some restaurants, too, are on offer here. The cable car leaves every half hour and you can ski, hike or wander around the top, or just go to an alpine café, and then ride back down. You can see lovely views of the Rositten Valley from the cable car. Staff at the departure point are very helpful and will advise you on routes or show you the paths on a map. **ⓐ** Dr. Friedrich Ödlweg 2 **ⓣ** 06246 724 770 **ⓦ** www.untersbergbahn.at **ⓛ** 09.00–17.00 Mar; 08.30–17.00 Apr–June & Oct; 08.30–17.30 July–Sept; 09.00–16.00 Dec–Feb. Admission charge

### Wasserspiele (Trick Fountains)

A marble table with a wine-cooler hole down the centre is the start of the tour of surprise water features in the Hellbrunn gardens. The prince used to surprise his guests or sober them up with splashes of water from such unexpected sources as seats. And so it goes on, around the grounds in a series of grottoes, statues and ponds, where the tour guide surprises all the visitors by starting up the spray jets. It is hilarious and you won't come away totally dry, they make sure of that. You can hear the squeals all round the grounds from unsuspecting visitors caught out in a shower. Look out for amusing moving figures and listen out for birdsong, all operated by ancient water mechanisms. They really are worth visiting. **ⓐ** Fürstenweg 37 **ⓣ** 0662 8203 720 **ⓛ** 09.00–16.30 Apr & Oct; 09.00–17.30 May,

June & Sept; 09.00–18.00 plus hourly tours of fountains until 22.00 July & Aug. Admission charge

## CULTURE

### Mechanical Theatre

Within the palace grounds at Hellbrunn make sure you take a look at the Mechanical Theatre. The stage is a mini Salzburg, showing figures from all the trades and daily life, from tailors to builders, court ladies, leather workers, street entertainers and butchers. All 250 wooden figures move, activated by water only. The wheels and cogs make rather a racket, so a hydraulic organ was also built to play classical music to mask some of the noise.

● *The Mechanical Theatre at Hellbrunn Palace is fully water-powered*

**Volkskundemuseum (Museum of Folk Art and Life)**
The museum is a short climb up steps into the beech woods on the hill behind the palace. It's housed in a so-called 'little castle' which the prince-archbishop had built as part of a wager; he claimed he could build it in less than a year. He won. You can see paintings depicting life in the area, such as various traditional costumes, decorated old wooden furniture, a collection of votive paintings and musical instruments as well as some gruesome masks, used in local customs and rituals to drive out bad spirits.
ⓐ Hellbrunner Monatsschlössl ⓛ 10.00–17.30. Admission charge

## TAKING A BREAK

**Café Anif £** Centrally located in the village of Anif and convenient as a stopping point for refreshments.
ⓐ Aniferstr. 11 ⓣ 06246 884 15 ⓛ 09.00–22.00 Mon–Sat

**Café Wegner £** A small and cosy café-cum-bar in the heart of Anif at the Niederalm crossroads. ⓐ Fürstenweg 1 ⓣ 06246 730 79
ⓛ 09.00–22.00 Mon–Wed, 09.00–00.00 Thur–Sat, 09.00–20.00 Sun

**Gasthaus zu Schloss Hellbrunn £** Not only is it a lovely setting in front of the palace, but the service and menu are good too. Come for an affordable lunch or just stop by for coffee and apple strudel.
ⓐ Fürstenweg 37 ⓣ 0662 825 608 ⓦ www.taste-gassner.com
ⓛ 11.30–17.30

**Kiosk at Schloss Hellbrunn £** There is a small snack point with a few tables and chairs at the entrance to the palace. You can get light snacks, coffees, drinks and ice creams here. ⏱ 09.00–17.30 May, June & Sept; 09.00–22.00 July & Aug

## AFTER DARK

### RESTAURANTS

**Atelier im Gasthaus zu Schloss Hellbrunn ££** This is the posh sister of the Gasthaus (left) and occupies the same building, but it is open only in the evenings. The Gault Millau-awarded gourmet restaurant serves a three-course vegetarian menu, a five-course surprise menu and a ten-course taster sampler. ⓐ Fürstenweg 37 ⓣ 0662 825 608 ⓦ www.taste-gassner.com ⏱ 18.30–23.00 Wed–Sat, June–Sept; 18.30–23.00 Thur–Sat, Apr, May & Oct

**Friesacher ££** Owned by the Friesacher family since 1846, this hotel and restaurant lies in idyllic grounds. Its gorgeous, largely wood-panelled interior is matched by an outdoor swimming pool and eating area. The prize winning restaurant serves traditional Austrian dishes with many of the ingredients supplied fresh from the family's own farm. ⓐ Hellbrunnerstr. 17, Anif ⓣ 06246 8977 ⓦ www.hotelfriesacher.com ⏱ 11.30–22.30

## ACCOMMODATION

**Hotel Gartenauer £** Beautifully located in the village of Anif just south of the city. Relax in the hotel's sauna or solarium; do a couple of lengths in the outdoor swimming pool; or get out and active enjoying a hike, playing the nearby golf course,

or a few sets of tennis. ⓐ Hellbrunnerstr. 7 ⓣ 06246 724 65
ⓦ www.gartenauer.at

**Hotel Untersberg £** A lovely chalet-style, family-run hotel at
the foot of Untersberg, right by the gondola. A great base if
you want to explore the mountain. It's just 7 km (4¹/₂ miles)
from the centre of Salzburg, and has a garden café, sauna,
solarium and even free bike hire. Modern, clean and friendly.
ⓐ Dr Friedrich Oedl-Weg 1, St Leonhard/Grödig ⓣ 06246 725 75
ⓦ www.hoteluntersberg.at

**Pension Christophorus Haus £** Located in Neu Anif, the newer
part of Anif, almost in Grödig. A very affordable guesthouse,
handy for cyclists and close to the bus stop. Ten rooms, some
with enclosed balconies. ⓐ Neu-Aniferstr. 2, Anif ⓣ 06246 729 71

**Advena Point Hotel Salzburg ££** In the countryside near the
Reschenbergweg bus stop. It's ten minutes from Salzburg centre,
ten minutes from the airport and close to the motorway exit.
Good for the sports oriented, as it offers guests a pool, sauna,
massage treatments, golf and tennis. ⓐ Eisgrabenstr. 32, Anif
ⓣ 06246 742 56 ⓦ www.advenahotels.com

**Hotel Schlosswirt ££** A 4-star hotel dating back to 1607 in the
centre of Anif village. Cosy rooms with some traditional and
historic furniture. It also has a beautiful dining room. The hotel
takes its name from the nearby castle. ⓐ Anif 22 ⓣ 06246 721 75
ⓦ www.schlosswirt-anif.com

# The Austrian Lakes: Wolfgangsee

Take in the breathtaking beauty of the alpine lake district and enjoy scenery from *The Sound of Music,* castles, hunting lodges, shimmering lakes and picturesque views. Wolfgangsee is one of the larger lakes, with a great number of activities for all ages and tastes. It's a true sporting paradise, with opportunities for both lake and mountain activities, such as skiing, cycling, waterskiing and paragliding. Whether you want to get active or just potter around villages with marvellous churches, it's a wonderful place to stay.

Wolfgangsee lies over 20 km (12¹/₂ miles) east of Salzburg in the region known as Salzkammergut (literally 'salt chamber estates') and can be reached by car or bus. The key towns on the lake are St Gilgen, St Wolfgang and Strobl. The mountains on either side of the lake provide yet more opportunities to get out and about, and wonderful views are simply everywhere. These are the foothills to the Alps.

On the way to Wolfgangsee, you pass Fuschlsee, another pretty lake. Fuschl itself is a beautiful town, especially in summer when lots of people camp here or stay in the many guesthouses at the lakeside. You can swim in the lakes and do watersports in summer, or skate on the lake and ski in the mountains in winter.

Visit the tourist information offices to book accommodation, get ideas and tips for trips, or find out about hot air ballooning, paragliding, cycling, waterskiing and snow skiing:

**St Gilgen** ⓐ Mondseebundesstr. 1A, near the Spar supermarket
ⓘ 06227 2348 ⓦ www.wolfgangsee.at

**St Wolfgang** Ⓐ Au 140, top end of town ① 06227 2348
Ⓦ www.wolfgangsee.at

## GETTING THERE

The buses in Salzburg operate only within the city area, so you
need to take a Post Bus to head out of town. Bus 150 leaves from
Mirabellplatz for Hof, Fuschl, St Gilgen and Strobl, with the end
destination Bad Ischl written on the front. Buy a return ticket from
the driver, which allows you to hop on and off as you please and
spend time in one of the places en route, or change buses. The 150
takes you to St Gilgen in 45 minutes. Have a look around, then take
either the boat across to St Wolfgang or another bus, which often
changes in Strobl. For more information and details, contact **ÖBB-
Postbus** (Ⓐ Andreas-Hofer-Str. 9 ① 0662 466 00 Ⓦ www.postbus.at).

If you go by car, drive along the right bank Linzer
Bundesstrasse out of town in a northeasterly direction. The
road becomes Grazer Bundesstr. and then B158 in the direction
of St Gilgen and St Wolfgang. It takes you past Fuschlsee and
on to St Gilgen. St Wolfgang lies on the other side of the lake,
so drive around the lake passing through Strobl.

> **TRAVEL TIP**
> A **Salzkammergut Erlebnis Card** (Salzkammergut Explorer
> Card) entitles you to lots of reductions on sights and
> transport in the region. You can check out details and
> prices on Ⓦ www.salzkammergut.at

⬤ The serene stillness of Wolfgangsee

A four-hour organised tour to the Salzkammergut region can be booked with **Panorama** (ⓦ www.panoramatours.com).

## SIGHTS & ATTRACTIONS

### Boat ride to St Gilgen or St Wolfgang

The fleet of boats on Wolfgangsee zig-zag across the lake, taking you between St Gilgen, Fürberg, Ried-Falkenstein (for Pfarrkirche, the Pilgrim's Church), Schafbergbahnhof (for the mountain railway), St Wolfgang, Gschwendt and Strobl. Check the prices and timetable online or get a timetable from the tourist information office in St Gilgen. If you are lucky, the old paddle steamer may be running in high summer. ⓐ Markt 35, St Wolfgang ⓣ 06138 223 20 ⓦ www.schafbergbahn.at

### Dorf der Tiere (Animal Village)

This zoo for small animals makes a nice outing for young children. There's also a playground and go-karts. ⓐ Adamgasse 3, Abersee ⓣ 0676 5336 748 ⓦ www.dorfdertiere.at ⓛ 09.30–19.00 Mar–Oct

### Schafbergbahn

The mountain railway up to Schafberg (Sheep Mountain) is fun for all the family as the little steam locomotive puffs and pushes the carriages up the mountain in good weather from July to September. More modern trains also operate between April and October. The railway starts in St Wolfgang and runs over 5 km (3 miles) to its mountain destination. Tickets are available in many combinations, including boat and railway, family, single journey, or even return journey with an overnight stay and breakfast at the hotel on the peak. ⓐ Markt 35, St Wolfgang ⓣ 06138 223 20 ⓦ www.schafbergbahn.at

## St Gilgen's Four Museums

The town of St Gilgen offers a special ticket to visit its little museums. The Heimatkundliches Museum (Local History Museum) informs you about lace makers, handicrafts, glassware and music of the region. The Mozarthaus is Mozart's mother's birthplace. She lived in St Gilgen before marrying Wolfgang Amadeus' father, and the composer's sister was married in the church here. The museum puts on a multimedia show of the Mozart family's life in English. The Zinkenbach Colony of Painters was a group in the 1920s and 30s who moved from Vienna to Wolfgangsee. Their work is honoured in the Museum der Zinkenbacher Malerkolonie. And, last but not least, the Musikinstrumente-Museum (Musical Instrument Museum) explores world folk musical instruments.

**Heimatkundliches Museum** ⓐ Pichlerplatz 6 ⓣ 06227 2642 ⓦ www.museum-sankt-gilgen.at ⓛ 10.00–12.00, 15.00–18.00 Tues–Sun, June–Sept

**Mozarthaus** ⓐ Ischler Str. 15 ⓣ 06227 2348 ⓦ www.mozartdorf.at ⓛ 10.00–12.00, 15.00–18.00 Tues–Sun, June–Sept

**Museum der Zinkenbacher Malerkolonie** ⓐ Aberseestr. 11 ⓣ 06767 430 916 ⓦ www.malerkolonie.at ⓛ 15.00–19.00 Tues–Sun, July–Sept

**Musikinstrumente-Museum** ⓐ Aberseestr. 11 ⓣ 06227 8235 ⓦ www.hoerart.at ⓛ 09.00–11.00, 15.00–19.00 Tues–Sun, June–Oct; 09.00–11.00, 14.00–17.00 Mon–Fri, Nov & Dec;

09.00–11.00, 15.00–18.00 Mon–Thur, 09.00–11.00 Fri,
15.00–18.00 Sun, Jan–May

### Zwölferhorn

Take the gondola up Twelve Horn Mountain (1,522 m/4,993 ft) from
St Gilgen to enjoy the views and hiking or cycling trails. It takes
just 16 minutes. In clear weather you can see alpine peaks for miles
around. Routes are well marked and suitable for the moderately
fit and families. There are also two inns and a few mountain
cottages, called Alm or Hütte, where you can get refreshments,
and a large café with a sun terrace at the gondola station.
ⓐ Konrad-Lesiak-Platz 3 ⓣ 06227 2350 ⓦ www.12erhorn.at
ⓛ 09.00–18.00 June–Aug; 09.00–17.00 Sept; 09.00–16.30 Oct

## CULTURE

### Pfarrkirche (Pilgrim Church)

Visit the 15th-century church in St Wolfgang where pilgrims
flocked in the late Middle Ages in a sort of early form of tourism.
It boasts the Pacher Altar, a magnificent late-Gothic masterpiece.
This winged altar is a wood carving of intricate detail. Outside
the church is the pilgrims' fountain from 1515. ⓐ Markt 18,
St Wolfgang ⓛ Services: 09.30 Sun, 14.30 Tues, 08.15 Wed,
19.00 Thur, 19.00 (18.00 in winter) Sat

## TAKING A BREAK

**Fischer Wirt £** A large restaurant with a terrace at the lakeside.
They specialise in fresh lake fish dishes but have good coffees and

snacks as well. Sit and watch the boats arriving and departing from the pier next door. ⓐ Ischlerstr. 21, St Gilgen ❶ 06227 2304 ⓦ www.fischer-wirt.at ❸ 09.00–late

**Schafbergspitze £** The hotel's restaurant or café terrace offers breakfast specials if you take an early train up, or evening meals to watch the sun set. Whatever the time of day, the views are magnificent. ⓐ Ried 23, St Wolfgang ❶ 0613 835 42 (May–Oct) ⓦ www.schafberg.net ❸ 24 hrs May–Oct

◐ *St Wolfgang nestles in the foothills of the Alps*

**Zum Weissen Hirschen £** This restaurant and café has a huge lakeside terrace for summer, and cosy rooms indoors. Watch the pedalos and small boats come and go at Uferplatz (the town's mooring place) while you sip a coffee or beer under the horse chestnuts. ⓐ Markt 73, St Wolfgang ⓣ 06138 2238 ⓦ www.weisserhirsch.at ⓛ 11.00–22.00

⬥ *Gasthof zur Post in St Gilgen*

## AFTER DARK

### RESTAURANTS

**Im Weissen Rössl ££** The White Horse Inn in the centre of
St Wolfgang was made famous in an operetta using its
name by Ralph Benatzky in 1930. The fun songs were about
the area, the weather and the people. ⓐ Markt 74, St Wolfgang
ⓣ 06138 230 60 ⓦ www.weissesroessl.at ⓛ 09.00–00.00

**Joseph's ££** A contemporary restaurant and wine bar with a fine
daily changing menu, and it's right in the heart of St Wolfgang.
ⓐ Markt 17, St Wolfgang ⓣ 06138 204 60 ⓦ www.josephs.at
ⓛ 17.30–22.30 Wed–Sat, 11.30–14.00 Fri–Sun

**Hotel Schloss Fuschl £££** This expensive hotel, fancy restaurant
and bar makes a lovely romantic place to have a drink in front of
the fireplace or, if you want to splash out on some 5-star luxury,
a meal with a view over Fuschlsee. Famous guests have included
Brigitte Bardot, Roger Moore and Romy Schneider. This former
hunting lodge of the prince-archbishops was renovated in 2006,
and now has several luxury lakeside cottages to rent. If you catch a
bus to your dinner venue, the bus stops close by, and you can enjoy
the walk down the sweeping drive to the castle at the lakeside.
ⓐ Schloss Str. 19, Hof ⓣ 06229 225 30 ⓦ www.schlossfuschlresort.at
ⓛ 11.00–22.00

### ACCOMMODATION

**Christerbauer £** A cute, affordable, family-run hotel with a little

garden and a restaurant serving regional specialities. It's in the centre of the town too. ⓐ Brunettiplatz 3, St Gilgen ⓣ 06227 204 57 ⓦ www.christerbauer.at

**Hotel Radetzky £** This hotel is smart and traditional but pleasant and comfortable. Contemporary stylish rooms and good food are on offer. ⓐ Streicherplatz 1, St Gilgen ⓣ 06227 2232 ⓦ www.hotelradetzky.at

**Hotel Schafbergspitze £** This place offers a unique overnight stay at 1,783 m (5,850 ft) above sea level. The rooms have showers and toilets and there's a kids' play area, restaurant with regional specialities and a terrace to enjoy the panorama. ⓐ Ried 23, St Wolfgang ⓣ 0613 835 42 (May–Oct) ⓦ www.schafberg.net

**Gasthof zur Post ££** The ancient exterior and 17th-century frescoes on the façade belie the stylish modern rooms inside. Excellent food and wine, and close to sights and the lakeside. ⓐ Mozartplatz 8, St Gilgen ⓣ 06227 2157 ⓦ www.gasthofzurpost.at

**Im Weissen Rössl ££–£££** A luxury hotel right in the heart of St Wolfgang with excellent restaurants and a spa and pool. It has lots of history and fame as the subject of the operetta *The White Horse Inn*. ⓐ Markt 74, St Wolfgang ⓣ 06138 230 60 ⓦ www.weissesroessl.at

ⓞ *Tour Salzburg on its well-connected public transport system*

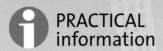

# PRACTICAL
## information

# Directory

## GETTING THERE

### By air

Several airlines fly into Salzburg, but some flights require a change at Frankfurt, Vienna or Munich. For airport details see ⓦ www.salzburg-airport.com. It is possible to fly to Munich Airport and book a transfer car or rail ticket. You can reach Salzburg from Munich in one and a half hours by train, and from Vienna in three hours. Online timetables and prices are available in English at ⓦ www.oebb.at

**Aer Lingus** (from Dublin) ⓦ www.aerlingus.com

**Austrian Arrows** (from London Heathrow) ⓦ www.aua.com

**British Airways** (from London Gatwick)
ⓦ www.britishairways.com

**British Midland** (from London Gatwick) ⓦ www.flybmi.com

**Jet2** (from Leeds) ⓦ www.jet2.com

**Lufthansa** (from London Heathrow) ⓦ www.lufthansa.at

**Ryanair** (from London Stansted) ⓦ www.ryanair.com

**Sky Europe** (from Manchester) ⓦ www.skyeurope.com

**Styrian Spirit** (from Birmingham) ⓦ www.styrianspirit.com

Many people are aware that air travel emits $CO_2$, which contributes to climate change. You may be interested in the possibility of lessening the environmental impact of your flight through the charity **Climate Care** (ⓦ www.climatecare.org), which offsets your $CO_2$ by funding environmental projects around the world.

### By rail

Trains arrive from all major European rail hubs at the central Hauptbahnhof (see page 50).

The monthly *Thomas Cook European Rail Timetable* has up-to-date schedules for European international and national train services. **Thomas Cook European Rail Timetable** ❶ (UK) 01733 416477, (USA) 1 800 322 3834 Ⓦ www.thomascookpublishing.com

## ENTRY FORMALITIES

Citizens of the UK, Republic of Ireland and other EU countries can visit for an unlimited time without a visa. Nationals of the USA, Canada, Australia and New Zealand do not require visas either and can enter Austria with a valid passport and stay up to three months. South African nationals require a passport and visa.

## MONEY

The unit of currency is the euro, which is divided into 100 cents. Banknotes have face values of 5, 10, 20, 50, 100, 200 and 500 euros. Coins come in 1 and 2 euro denominations as well as 1, 2, 5, 10, 20 and 50 cents. Foreign currency can be exchanged at any commercial bank, such as **Raiffeisen Bank** (❷ Sigmund-Haffner-Gasse). Banks are closed on Saturdays and Sundays, but bureaux de change at airports and rail terminals are open seven days a week. The Bank of Austria has two handy ATMs in Getreidegasse and Churfürststrasse, near Café Tomaselli. Major credit and debit cards are widely accepted, but some of the smaller hotels and restaurants may only accept cash.

**Bureaux de change:**
**Central Station Western Union, Österreichische**
**Verkehrskreditbank** @ Südtiroler Platz 1 ☎ 0662 871 377
🕐 08.30–19.00 Mon–Fri, 08.30–14.30 Sat
**Interchange Austria** @ Mozartplatz 5 ☎ 0676 8404 3617
🕐 09.00–18.00 Mon–Fri, 10.00–14.00 Sat
**Salzburger Sparkasse Airport** @ Innsbrucker Bundesstr. 95
☎ 050 1004 7636 🕐 08.00–16.00
**Salzburg Airport Information Counter** Offers additional exchange
facilities after business hours. @ Innsbrucker Bundesstr. 95
🕐 05.00–23.00

## HEALTH, SAFETY & CRIME

Salzburg water is of premium quality and it can be drunk from
the taps without fear of repercussions. Medical facilities in the
city are excellent and enough people are English-speaking to
ensure that you'll be able to explain the nature of any symptoms
or ailments without a problem. Visitors to rural or forest areas
in spring and summer should take precautions against tick
infestation. Chemists can be found at Fürsterzbischöfliche
Hofapotheke, Alter Markt or Biberapotheke Getreidegasse.

Crime levels are fairly low in Salzburg, on a par with other
small European towns and cities. A small number of police do
wander around the city, recognisable in their blue uniforms.

## OPENING HOURS

Shops and businesses are usually open 09.00 or 10.00–18.00
Monday to Friday and 09.00–17.00 Saturday. Some smaller

## MEDICAL INSURANCE

Medical costs are high so visitors are advised to obtain sufficient comprehensive medical insurance for their stay, whether as part of their travel insurance or separately. Ensure you keep any receipts for medical treatment. You will usually be required to pay via a bank transfer; credit cards are not accepted. European nationals should obtain the European Health Insurance Card (EHIC) before leaving home. This allows access to free or subsidised state-provided medical treatment. For more information in Britain, see
🌐 www.direct.gov.uk

places may open at 08.00 and close for lunch between 12.30 and 14.30. Souvenir shops may open on Sundays and public holidays. Banks are normally open 08.00–12.00, 13.00–17.00 Monday to Wednesday, 08.00–12.00, 13.00–16.30 Thursday, and 08.00–13.00 Friday.

## TOILETS

These are clean and modern on the whole, especially in public buildings, museums and historical sights. You can also nip into cafés and restaurants. Public toilets are located at various points around the centre, including Makartsteg and Staatsbrücke on the right bank, between the Dom and Erzabtei St Peter, at the Altstadt Garagen, Franz-Josef Park, Mirabell Gardens, next to the Dreifaltigkeitskirche, and at the Hauptbahnhof.

## CHILDREN

Some hotels provide a baby phone and baby cot and most restaurants are child friendly. DM drugstore on Universitätsplatz is a good place to buy baby food and things like dummies and nappies. Most public toilets in larger restaurants or museums have nappy changing facilities.

In terms of entertainment, Salzburg has a lot to offer children. The following are some of the most popular activities:

### Eisarena Salzburg (Ice Rink)

In Volksgarten Park. ⓐ Leopoldskronstr. 50 ⓣ 0662 829 265
ⓛ 10.00–16.15 early Oct–end Mar ⓝ Bus: 6, 7, 20.
Admission charge

### Erlebnispark Strasswalchen

This is a huge adventure park, northeast of the city, which takes an hour to reach by car (see the website for map). If you catch a bus or train (get details from the Hauptbahnhof), you'll be given a discount on the entry price when you show your travel ticket. There are plenty of train and boat rides once you get there, a magic show and restaurants. ⓐ Märchenweg 1, Strasswalchen ⓣ 06215 8181 ⓦ www.erlebnispark.at
ⓛ 10.00–18.00 end April–end Oct

### Europark Kids' Club

The out-of-town shopping centre has a two-storey adventure playground for kids. ⓐ Europastr. 1, PF 24 ⓣ 0662 4420 210
ⓦ www.europark.at ⓛ 09.00–19.30 Mon–Fri, 09.00–18.00 Sat
ⓝ Bus: 1

⬥ *Take the funicular up to Festung Hohensalzburg*

### Festung Hohensalzburg

The funicular up to the fortress is fun and its courtyards provide lots of space to run around. Older kids will love the treasures, masks and weapons in the museum. ⓐ Mönchsberg 34 ⓣ 0662 8424 3011 ⓦ www.salzburg-burgen.at ⓛ 09.30–17.00 Oct–Apr; 09.00–19.00 May–Sept. Admission charge

### *Fiaker*

Kids will love a ride in a horse-drawn carriage from Domplatz. ⓦ www.fiaker-salzburg-benkoe.at

### Freilichtmuseum (Open-air Museum)

Austria's rural open-air museum is southeast of the city. See old-fashioned country life. ⓐ 8114 Stübing ⓣ 03124 537 00 ⓦ www.freilichtmuseum.at ⓛ 09.00–17.00 Tues–Sun. Admission charge

## Haus der Natur (Natural History Museum)

Reptiles, dinosaurs and lots of interactive displays in no fewer than 80 exhibition rooms. Watch the mini sharks being fed in the aquarium. ⓐ Museumsplatz 5 ❶ 0662 842 653 ⓦ www.hausdernatur.at ❸ 09.00–17.00, reptile zoo: 10.00–17.00. Admission charge

## Hellbrunn

Trick fountains, an adventure playground, loads of space, and even a zoo. ⓐ Fürstenweg 37 ❶ 0662 820 3720 ❸ 09.00–16.30 Apr & Oct; 09.00–17.30 May, June & Sept; 09.00–22.00 July & Aug. Admission charge

## Spielzeugmuseum (Toy Museum)

Austria's only toy museum. ⓐ Bürgerspitalgasse 2 ❶ 0662 62080 8300 ⓦ www.salzburgmuseum.at ❸ 09.00–17.00

## Swimming

When the weather's hot, head to the city's open-air pools. In poor weather stick to the indoor Paracelsus (see page 36). **Freibad Alpenstrasse** ⓐ Alpenstr. ❶ 0662 620 832 ❸ 09.00–19.00/20.00 mid-May–Sept. Admission charge **Freibad Leopoldskron** ⓐ Leopoldskronstr. 50 ❶ 0662 829 265 ❸ 07.00–20.00 ❶ Opening times depend on weather conditions. Admission charge **Freibad Volksgarten** ⓐ Hermann-Bahr-Promenade 2 ❶ 0662 62341 14347 ❸ 09.00–19.00/20.00 May & Sept; 09.00–22.00 Sun–Thur, 09.00–23.30 Fri & Sat, June–Aug. Admission charge

## COMMUNICATIONS

### Internet

Offering internet access, discount phone booths for international calls, and phonecards.

**City Net Café** ⓐ Gstättengasse 11, near Mönchsberg Lift
ⓘ 0662 841 672 ⓛ 10.00–22.00 ⓝ Bus: 1, 4

### Phone

You can make overseas direct calls from internet cafés (see above) and public telephone boxes. The latter are normally two together, one accepting coins (10 cents, 20 cents, 50 cents, €1 and €2) where the minimum is 30 cents, the other accepting pre-paid phonecards.

### TELEPHONING SALZBURG

To call Salzburg from abroad, dial the international access code (usually 00), Austria's country code 43 and Salzburg's area code 662, followed by the local number. To call Salzburg from within Austria, dial 0662.

**Directory enquiries for Austria and Europe** 118 877

### TELEPHONING ABROAD

To make long-distance calls from Austria, dial 00 plus the country code, then the local area code (dropping the 0), then the local number. Some country codes :

Australia 61   Canada 1   France 33   Germany 49
Japan 81   Netherlands 31   New Zealand 64
South Africa 27   United Kingdom 44   United States 1

**International directory enquiries** 0900 118 877

You can buy phonecards at internet cafés and some kiosks, in denominations of €3.60 and €6.90. Telephone boxes are pale or dark grey booths, with or without doors. Collect calls to the USA, Canada, UK, Germany and Japan are possible, as well as credit card calls to all countries, by calling 0800 008 014. Dial 1 at the prompt to hear English. Austria's mobile network operates on the 900 and 1800 bands for GSM, and the main provider is A1. For more information visit Ⓦ www.telekom.at

## Post
Postal services are efficient and swift. A standard letter takes approx 2–3 days within Europe. Post boxes are emptied Monday to Friday until 17.00. Post boxes on walls or posts around the city are yellow and marked 'Post'. Staff at the post offices speak a little English or will find you someone who can.
**PO Old Town left bank** ⓐ Residenzplatz 9 Ⓛ 07.00–18.30 Mon–Fri, 08.00–10.00 Sat
**PO Old Town right bank** ⓐ Makartplatz 6 Ⓛ 07.30–18.00 Mon–Fri

## ELECTRICITY
The electrical supply is 220 V, 50 Hz. European round, two-pin plugs are standard. British, Australian and South African visitors need a plug adaptor, available at airport shops, electrical stores and most department stores. Americans and Canadians with 110 V equipment will need a transformer as well as an adaptor.

## TRAVELLERS WITH DISABILITIES
The tourist information office produces a good guide and map to the city for visitors with disabilities: *Salzburg Barrierefrei Erleben*

('Experiencing Salzburg without Obstacles'). It lists all accessible sights, venues and hotels. Get a copy sent by post prior to travelling or pick one up in the Salzburg tourist information office. Contact the commissioner for people with disabilities for further information (❶ 0662 8072 3232 ❷ 08.00–16.00 Mon–Thur, 08.00–12.00 Fri ❸ behindertenbeauftragte@stadt-salzburg.at).

## TOURIST INFORMATION

Tourist information offices will provide free maps, hotel booking for a nominal fee, and advice. They have endless brochures and leaflets in English on all the sights, attractions and events. The staff are all extremely helpful, speak very good English and know their city inside out. The general website is vast and very thorough.

The *Salzburger Nachrichten* is another helpful resource and can be bought from any kiosk. It tells you what's going on in the city daily, but only comes out in German. Their website has an English version (❿ www.salzburg.com). Other free publications can be picked up from hotel lobbies, venues and tourist information offices. The *Top of Salzburg City Guide* has addresses for places to eat and drink, and *Shopping Eating Art in Salzburg* is produced in English and German by the marketing organisation Altstadt Salzburg.

**Tourist Board Salzburg Information** ❶ 0662 889 870
❿ www.salzburg.info
**Tourist Information Hauptbahnhof** ❹ Bahnsteig 2A
❶ 0662 8898 7340
**Tourist Information Mozartplatz** Event tickets can be booked here. ❹ Mozartplatz 5 ❶ 0662 8898 7330
**Tourist Information Salzburg Airport** ❹ Innsbrucker Bundesstr. 95

# Emergencies

The following are emergency free-call numbers:

**Ambulance** 🛈 144     **Euro-emergency** 🛈 112

**Fire** 🛈 122     **Medical emergency** 🛈 141

**Police** 🛈 133

## MEDICAL SERVICES

**Medicent** A modern, general centre with doctors, dentists, specialists for women and children, plus a chemist and parking. Call to make an appointment. It's located out of the centre. ⓐ Innsbrucker Bundesstr. 35 🛈 0662 901 00 🅦 www.medicentsalzburg.com ⏰ 08.00–19.00 Mon–Fri Ⓝ Bus: 1, 2, 20, 28

**Landesnervenklinik (Christian Doppler Neuroclinic)** ⓐ Ignaz-Harrer-Str. 79 🛈 0662 448 30 Ⓝ Bus: 4, 24, 32

**Landeskrankenhaus Salzburg (St Johanns Spital Regional Hospital)** ⓐ Müllner Hauptstr. 48 🛈 0662 448 20 🅦 www.lks.at Ⓝ Bus: 2, 4

**Unfallkrankenhaus Salzburg (Accident & Emergency Hospital)** ⓐ Dr Franz Rehrl Platz 5 🛈 0662 658 00 ⏰ A&E: 24 hrs; visitors: 10.00–19.00; outpatients: 07.00–12.00 Ⓝ Bus: 6, 49

## POLICE

There is a police help point at the Hauptbahnhof (railway station) on the right bank and the Rathaus (town hall) on the left bank.
**Police headquarters** ⓐ Alpenstr. 90 🛈 0591 335 50

## EMBASSIES & CONSULATES

Further information is available from the Austrian consulate in your country or from the website of the **Austrian Ministry**

---

**EMERGENCY PHRASES**

| **Help!** | **Fire!** | **Stop!** |
|---|---|---|
| Hilfe! | Feuer! | Halt! |
| *Heelfe!* | *Foyer!* | *Halt!* |

**Please call an ambulance/a doctor/the police/the fire service!**
Rufen Sie bitte einen Krankenwagen/einen Arzt/
die Polizei/die Feuerwehr!
*Roofen zee bitter inen krankenvaagen/inen artst/
dee politsye/dee foyervair!*

---

of Foreign Affairs (Ⓦ www.bmaa.gv.at).

**Australian Embassy** ⓐ Mattiellistr. 2–4, Vienna ⓣ 01 506 740
Ⓦ www.australian-embassy.at

**Canadian Embassy** ⓐ Laurenzerberg 2, Vienna ⓣ 01 531 383 000

**New Zealand Consulate-General** ⓐ Salesianergasse 15/3, Vienna
ⓣ 01 3188 505

**South African Honorary Consulate Salzburg** ⓐ Buchenweg 14,
Elsbethen-Glasenbach ⓣ 0662 622 035 ⓛ 15.00–17.00 Mon–Thur

**South African Embassy** ⓐ Sandgasse 33, Vienna ⓣ 01 3206 493

**UK Consulate** (for Great Britain and Northern Ireland) ⓐ Alter
Markt 4, Salzburg ⓣ 0662 848 133 ⓛ 09.00–11.30 Mon–Fri

**UK Embassy** ⓐ Jauresgasse 12, Vienna ⓣ 01 716 130
Ⓦ www.usembassy.at

**US Embassy** ⓐ Boltzmanngasse 16, Vienna ⓣ 01 313 390

Editorial/project management: Lisa Plumridge
Copy editor: Paul Hines
Layout/DTP: Alison Rayner

The publishers would like to thank the following individuals and organisations for supplying their copyright photographs for this book: Foto Casino Austria, page 32; Pictures Colour Library, pages 73, 87 & 127; Salzburger Information, pages 10, 19, 42–3, 67, 83 & 91; Wolfgangsee Tourismus Gesellschaft, page 124; World Pictures, page 123; Caroline Jones, all others.

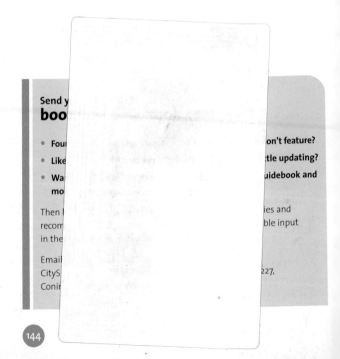

Send y
**boo**

- Fou
- Like
- Wa
  mo

Then
recom
in the

Email
CityS
Conir

on't feature?
tle updating?
uidebook and

ies and
ble input

227,